STRAWBERRY   POINT

STRAWBERRY POINT

Vignettes of an Iowa Childhood

By

Florence Roe Wiggins

Publishers

T. S. DENISON & COMPANY, INC.

Minneapolis

Copyright ©, 1967, by
FLORENCE ROE WIGGINS

International Copyright Secured
Library of Congress Catalog Card Number: 67-20671

DEDICATION

For Patty, Bruce, Candi and Chad who, born and reared in the shadow of Hollywood, have given delighted and wide-eyed attention to this chronicle of the simple life of Yesterday—a story as remote from and foreign to their own experiences as any Arabian Nights' tale, and to them, equally fantastic.

ACKNOWLEDGMENT

Portions of this book originally appeared as essays in *The Christian Science Monitor, The Annals of Iowa, The Iowan,* and *Harvest Years.*

Gratitude is lovingly tendered to Miss Ida Mae Hoag of Thoburn Terrace, Alhambra, California, for her assistance in recalling important details of many childhood experiences. Mrs. Pearl Hoag Steinhilber (now deceased) rendered excellent help in the recollection of dates, events and names. The diary of my grandfather, Marion Hoag, has been most helpful and the Journal of my uncle, Charles Roe, has been invaluable in supplying information about his father's first trip to Iowa in 1851 and in recalling accurately the events on the automobile trip through Iowa in 1903.

The passage in the ENVOY beginning "I walked down a country lane" . . . and ending "such a home expresses a permanence" is from A CASE FOR THE COUNTRY published in *The Christian Science Monitor,* February 2, 1963. It is reprinted by the kind permission of The Christian Science Publishing Society.

Gratitude, too, is due the many readers of The Christian Science Monitor who have expressed the desire that these essays be published in book form.

A HERITAGE FOR CANDICE LEE

If, to my daughter's daughter, I would bring
A heritage of value — of lasting delight,
Then, from my own inheritance, I would choose
The treasures shelved quite often out of sight.

We seldom talked about this priceless wealth
My mother's mother loved and gave to me,
But I was early taught to value it —
Her love for quiet ways — simplicity.

* * * * *

I treasure the promise of rose-bright dawn,
The silence of twilight time,
The warmth, the cheer, of hearth-fire glow,
My tall clock's loud-voiced chime,
A tea table gleaming with candle light,
The scent of blossoms, the gold-orange sight
In this always-summer clime.

I treasure the fragrance of fresh-baked bread,
A kitchen shiningly clean,
Sunbeams dancing on braided rugs,
A wise Siamese, the queen,
Who, except for a daffodill,
Reigns alone on the window sill,
And owns the whole cuisine.

* * * * *

Flowers, music, firelight, books — bring deep
Content. Our progressive age may see
A different world, Yet, I would keep this way
Of life, a heritage, for Candice Lee.

Florence Roe Wiggins

CONTENTS

* Reprinted by permission from The Christian Science Monitor.
© 1962, 1963, 1964 The Christian Science Publishing Society.
All rights reserved.

A NOTE TO THE READER

These vignettes of life in Iowa at the turn of the century are the result of the interested listening that I have been doing as my children and their friends have aired their problems in my presence. (Often around the kitchen table at snack time or as they lounged evenings in front of the grate fire in my living room.) These thinking young people, now in their late thirties, who were born into a topsy-turvy world and have courageously fought two devastating wars, have been asking themselves hard questions — questions they have found difficulty in answering.

"What has happened to the qualities that made our country great?" they ask. "What were they, anyway?" "What did those men of yesterday have in the way of stamina that we lack today? Did they possess more courage, fortitude, initiative than we do? How is it that they were able to order their lives while we seem to have so little control over ours? Why do we allow ourselves to be pushed onto a treadmill or into a 'rat-race?' Why have we become just cogs in a giant wheel, just 'numbers' in huge plants and factories of 20,000 employees? Is all this really Progress? What is happening to our individualities? Do we think too much of security or do we have the wrong idea of what security is?" These are the questions Young America is asking itself.

For the past thirty years I have been keenly interested in the early history of our country and have traced over a hundred families back to their immigrant ancestors. Because of this I am aware of the fact that the answers to all of these questions can be found in the lives of the men and women who founded our country and in the lives of their descendants down to the present century.

In writing the story of the Roes and the Hoags, I have made no effort to point out these answers, but they are there. I have been careful to write them between the lines, and it is there they will have to be read. I have tried not to be nostalgic. To look back longingly to the "good old days" is foolish, or at least unprogressive. Lot's wife taught us that. But it does seem wisdom to prize the treasure that is our heritage, and to incorporate it into our own lives.

The debt we owe our forebears is summed up tersely and forcibly in the Preface to the Eddy Genealogy:

> "If the America we love continues her favored way among the nations, it will ever be because of those very qualities woven into the fabric of our nation's life by our ancestors in old New England. Thence springs the path for Liberty's sure progress on the earth. Thence burns the clear flame, the reverence for God, that has lifted the Anglo-Saxon race to world leadership."

Florence Roe Wiggins
Laguna Beach, California

1

STRAWBERRY POINT

IN 1893, AMERICA emerged from the tinsel and wonder of the World's Fair in Chicago to drop immediately into such a depression and panic as it had never experienced before. Soup kitchens were installed in Chicago, and the lines of miserable and wretched unemployed grew longer all through the severe winter of 1893 - 94. Coxey's Army assembled early in the spring of 1894 and made its unsuccessful march on Washington. Strikes were the order of the day and city newspapers were calling for funds to feed the starving women and children.

Less than two hundred miles west of Chicago, in its beautiful

setting of rolling hills and fruitful fields, lay the quiet, self-sufficient little Iowa town, where I spent my childhood — Strawberry Point. No radios blasted out the tales of unemployment
and starvation in the nearby cities. There were no automobiles
and no highways to drive them on; no planes to disturb the
quiet of the heavens, and at that time there were not even telephones in this village. Quite unaware of depressions, or even
the rest of the world, the town went quietly about its daily
living, secure, serene, and well supported by the fertile farms
around it.

The winter of 1893 Papa went to his father, who owned a
large farm about four miles from town, to borrow money.
Father was a photographer, and the town's one little studio was
for sale. The amount of money needed for the venture was the
sizable sum of five hundred dollars. Grandfather Roe was a
good business man when it came to marketing the produce
from his two hundred acre farm, but the vanities of life held
no interest for him. Not a word was said about "hard times,"
not a word to indicate it was a hazardous time to go into
business. Grandfather could see only one objection.

"But George," he remonstrated, "what will you do when
all the people in town have had their pictures taken?"

Evidently Father's explanation satisfied Grandfather, for he
got the loan. Prosperity was not supposed to have returned to
the country until 1899, but by 1898 my enterprising parents
not only had paid their debt to Grandfather but had saved
five hundred dollars more. This they used as a down payment
on a home of their own — a home completely free of debt when
the new century arrived two years later. In that unenlightened

era a mortgage was shunned as a plague, and no home-owner breathed freely until the ogre of debt was completely vanquished.

Strawberry Point took its name from a triangular-shaped patch of wild strawberries at the west end of Main Street. This broad, tree-lined street, skirted by comfortable homes, meandered leisurely down hill to the business district at the "Four Corners." From there it continued east to the well-kept little cemetery, situated on a high knoll at the east end of town. (To stroll out there on a Sunday afternoon was considered an ideal diversion.) At the Four Corners, Main Street was met by Elkader Street which came from the north and by South Street which true to its name came from the south, passing the schoolhouse on its way up town.

Elkader Street, named for the town of Elkader, the county seat of Clayton County, had the doubtful distinction of harboring on its west side all the saloons and pool halls of the town. They straggled down the block from the Four Corners to the railroad tracks, and no lady who valued her reputation was ever known to walk on that side of the street. Beyond the tracks the street gained respectability as Dr. Howard's large, Victorian house came to view. Situated on a little hill, this hospitable home not only offered its spacious, high-ceilinged rooms to all worthwhile town affairs, but donated the high ground behind the house as well. Howard's Hill was the town's official setting for shooting off fireworks on the Fourth of July, as well as the scene of numerous tobogganing parties during the long winter months.

The Franklin Hotel, the pride of the town, stood at the Four

Corners. I doubt that it was built as early as 1893, but as far back as I can remember it was an important landmark. Uncle Fraze and Aunt Alma managed the hotel during all the years of my childhood and my parents and I were always welcome and privileged guests there. Every parade, in fact every event of any importance which took place on the streets of the town, we viewed from the large bay window of the public parlors on the second floor. From that vantage point we could see far down the streets in all four directions.

Aunt Alma's private sitting room, with its large windows on the south and east, overlooked East Main street and was the room I loved the best. Comfortable, bright and cheerful, it seemed to send out a special welcome to a little girl. In this pleasant room, with the kindly help of this loving aunt, I first learned to hold a tatting shuttle and make my first picot.

Cousin "Dory," another niece of Aunt Alma's, reigned supreme in the hotel's kitchen. Not even Aunt Alma gave orders to Dory. Her word was LAW and we all kept well out of her way when she was cooking for her "transients." She was as temperamental as any artist and justly proud of her culinary skill. Probably it was Dory's cooking even more than the clean, comfortable rooms that made the hotel so popular. Salesmen from the surrounding territory would plan, and sometimes drive their teams many long miles, to spend their Sundays at "The Franklin."

The hotel bore the name that the town had tried very hard to make its own. When the railroad arrived it was thought that the town should have a more dignified name than "Strawberry Point." Franklin was chosen and painted on signs at either end of the station building (we called it a depot). But the town fathers and the Milwaukee Railroad reckoned without human nature. Strawberry Point the town had been for twenty-five years, and Strawberry Point it continued to be.

After a few months' trial the signs on the depot came down and the conductor on the one daily train ceased singing, "All out for Franklin" to the passengers who continued to sit unconcernedly in their seats. (They were going to Strawberry Point.) Hard as the name is to say and undignified as it may be, Strawberry Point it has remained. But to those who know the town and love it best it will always be "The Point."

2

GRANDFATHER TURNED DOWN CHICAGO

ABOUT a year before the little town of Strawberry Point
came into existence Grandfather Roe made his first trip
to Iowa. It was on that memorable journey that he was offered
the trade — the Chicago Loop for his team and wagon!
Values were certainly different back in 1851.

Spring that year arrived in the Middle West in soggy attire.
Every day brought heavy thunder showers and the rivers and
streams were swollen to flood-like proportions. Grandfather
Roe, although young in years, twenty-six, was already old in
responsibilities. He had sold his farm near Buchanan, Michigan,
and was hoping to move his wife and family of three little girls

into the newly opened territory of northeastern Iowa. There was no railroad beyond Elgin, Illinois, at that time and to travel by covered wagon through unsettled country while rains were flooding the country-side seemed to him a dangerous and hazardous undertaking.

Early in April Grandfather's father, brother Lawson, and a cousin, William Roe, suddenly decided to join him on the trek into Iowa. The four men took Grandfather's wagon, equipped and ready for the trip. Leaving their families behind, they set out to make a preliminary survey of the new land. If the country lived up to their expectations, they would buy farms and then return to Michigan for their families.

In the sparsely settled country through which they travelled there were very few bridges and the horses were obliged to swim across most of the rivers. Each stream was tested as to depth and swiftness of current by riding the taller horse into the water. If he was able to keep his footing, the men would tie his whiffle-tree back to the wagon and let him pull it across while the smaller horse swam by his side. Many times the wagon box had to be tied to the running gear to keep it from floating away, and sometimes rafts had to be built to ferry the wagon and supplies across. It took three weeks of this slow travel for them to reach Chicago. (Today an excellent highway connects Buchanan, Michigan, to Chicago and the trip is a pleasant, two-hour drive.)

Since Grandfather did not want to drive down into the heart of the city, he tied his team to a fence between what was then the business district and the lake — about where State Street is today. Even then Chicago had reached a population of almost 30,000 and was growing fast — but not toward the lake. All the land bordering the lake and the river was little better than a swamp. As the four men walked up to the town to replenish their supplies, they noticed a farmer working in a field. When they returned he was waiting for them at the fence.

"Howdy, Strangers," he greeted them. "You folks amin' to settle hereabouts?"

"No," answered Grandfather pleasantly. "We're on our way to Iowa."

In spite of the travellers' evident lack of interest the man began to talk persuasively about the advantages of locating near such a fast growing city as Chicago. His oratory was convincing and he held his little audience spellbound until he confidently closed his sales talk by offering to trade forty acres of his farm on the lake front for their team, harness and wagon.

Grandfather was provoked. "What! Trade my strawberry roans, harness and wagon for this swamp land?" he said, with a sweep of his hand toward the lake. "I should say *not*. That would be a bad deal for me."

And the coming Loop District of Chicago was turned down without a moment's hesitation or a single qualm.

Three more weeks of tedious travel brought the men to the "Promised Land" — Delaware County, Iowa. This rolling country in the northeastern corner of the state was "beautiful for situation" with its low hills, wide valleys and rushing, spring-fed streams of water. Along the bottom lands of the rivers grew an abundance of timber,—black walnut, hickory, maple and elm trees. And best of all in the eyes of these four travel-weary farmers was the virgin soil, rich and black, holding

27

promise of fertility beyond their fondest hopes. All four men bought farms in the neighborhood. Great-Grandfather's was the largest and boasted a deep spring of water, icy cold and crystal clear — a spring that never faltered during the forty years that the farm stayed in the family.

The men lost no time, after their business was attended to, in starting on the return trip to Michigan. The first night, just at dusk, they reached the Maquoqueta River near the little town of Delaware. The river was high and the current so swift that the travellers decided not to attempt a crossing that night. Camp was made on a high knoll on the river bank.

A hard thunderstorm broke in the night and when daylight arrived, the men found their camp completely surrounded by water so deep it was impossible to get the wagon ashore. The horses were set free to make their own way to safety and the men took refuge in the wagon which they had fastened to a large oak tree. All too soon the rising waters forced them to abandon the wagon and climb into the tree.

By this time the farmers who lived along the river's edge had gathered on the banks but there seemed little they could do. No boat was available and the situation momentarily grew more critical. Suddenly one young farmer had an inspiration. By calking the few cracks in his new wagon box, he found to his satisfaction that it would float. Going upstream a short distance, this resourceful lad launched his makeshift boat and, using a board for a rudder, guided it to the tree where the men were marooned. He took two of them ashore, repeated the perilous trip and the rescue was complete.

(Sixty years later, on a Florida train, Uncle Charles was to have the pleasant experience of meeting his father's rescuer. As they visited together about pioneer days in Iowa, the stranger began to recount a story that Uncle immediately recognized as the rescue at the Maquoqueta River that he had heard his father tell so often. Uncle Charles interrupted, saying, "Wait, let me tell *you* the rest of that story." When Uncle finished, the elderly man exclaimed, "And I was the lad who took them all ashore!")

The remainder of the trip back to Michigan that spring of 1851 was comparatively uneventful. The journey back took another five weeks, but even at that they travelled faster than the stagecoach, for the letters written to their families while they were still in Iowa did not arrive until after the men reached Michigan.

The move to Iowa was made that summer. Two years later, Grandfather traded his eighty acres in Delaware County for the homestead rights of a large farm in Clayton County, four miles from the little town of Strawberry Point.

Even though Grandfather's team and wagon are long since gone and the Loop with its promise of fame and fortune lives on, yet we who were privileged to grow up in Strawberry Point instead of the "Windy City" have never regretted that Grandfather turned down Chicago.

3

WHEN TILLAGE BEGINS

"When tillage begins, other arts follow. The farmers therefore are the founders of human civilization."
Remarks on Agriculture by Daniel Webster

WHEN tillage began on Grandfather's farm the spring of 1853 the work was shared by every member of the household but Grandpa himself set an example that was hard to equal. His industry and his ability are as proverbial as were his grandfather's before him.

This ancestor, Charles Roe, for whom Grandfather was named, thoroughly enjoyed the freedom and the challenge of pioneer living. He was a skilled woodsman, a capable farmer and a shoemaker. One of the stories handed down from generation to generation relates that in one day he made a pair of shoes, thirty sugar troughs and helped with a barn raising!

Born at Oyster Bay, Long Island, five years before the Revolution, Charles arrived in a troubled world. His grandfather, Charles Feake, was an avowed royalist. His father, William Roe, just as ardent a patriot. Feeling ran strong in households with as divided loyalties as the Feakes and the Roes.

After the battle of Long Island was fought in August, 1776, and the British were so victorious that New York remained in their hands until the close of the war, William Roe became a spy. For almost two years his "underground" was successful but when at last his active support of the Colonies was discovered he was forced to "flee for his life."*

Mary Feake Roe lived on in the enemy country, caring for her six small children. (Two were younger than Charles.) Her position with her family as well as in the community was far from enviable. Her father was one of the 1300 men who signed the loyalist petition after the battle of Long Island. Her attractive and out-spoken aunt, Sarah Feake Cozzens, who was in Boston at the time war was declared, hurried back to the safety of Oyster Bay. Tradition says that she drank her tea too "conspicuously" while she was living in Boston.

In May, 1782, after four long years of separation from his family, William returned to Long Island under a flag of truce. He moved his wife and children "to ye main shore" and there, near Stamford, Connecticut, they established a temporary home. But their happiness at being a reunited family was all too brief. In December of that year William was taken prisoner by the Hessian hirelings of the British Army and didn't gain release until after the war was over.

*Roe-Platts Genealogy by Clarence A. Torrey

Both the Feake and Roe families were of long standing in the New World. William's great-grandfather, David Roe, arrived from England about 1666. The immigrant ancestor of the Feake family, Lieutenant Robert Feake, came with the Winthrop Fleet in 1630. (He married, the following year, Elizabeth Fones Winthrop, the fearless, spirited niece of Governor Winthrop) Pioneering and the love of adventure were bred in the very fibre of both William and Mary Roe. After the War of Independence it seemed not at all strange that they should turn their faces toward the new country opening up before them.

Kentucky was then the favored new frontier, a land of rich soil, of game and fish, of forests and clear running rivers. Best of all, bounties of land were available for soldiers who had served the Colonies. William Roe decided to take advantage of this opportunity. In 1787 (five years before Kentucky became a state) he, with his family and five slaves, settled in what was later known as Mason County. At that time it was "dangerous Indian Country" and the Roes were not spared the lurking perils of this newly opened territory.

Charles was a tall lad of sixteen when the move to Kentucky was made. He adapted quickly to the new life and soon learned to handle an axe and do a man's work. In 1794 he married Barsheba Watson, the gay, light-hearted daughter of Michael Watson who was a close friend and neighbor of the Roes.

The year of their marriage was the year that General Wayne won his decisive victory over the Indians and his treaty secured peace for all the land known as "The Northwestern Territory." As a result of that treaty rapid immigration followed. Charles and his sixteen year-old bride were eager to join the westward movement but parental disapproval dampened their enthusiasm. Charles was persuaded to buy one hundred acres of land near his father's plantation on the north fork of the Licking River.

Five children arrived during the next ten years, but the cares of motherhood rested lightly on easy-going Barsheba. She had an abundance of help. Her parents' slaves as well as those belonging to the Roes all considered it a privilege to be loaned to "Miss Bahsheba." The care-free young couple seldom missed the social life of the neighborhood — the parties, picnics, quilting bees, house and barn raisings — riding horseback wherever they went. Barsheba, especially, was very fond of riding and would dash out along the wooded paths on the fine, black horse kept for her exclusive use.

But this life did not satisfy the pioneer spirit of Charles Roe. The young couple's dream of adventure had never been completely abandoned and in 1804 they sold their land and with their five children (Watson was a baby not quite two) they joined a migration into Ohio. A few years later they moved again into the wild, raw country of Wayne County, Indiana — a wilderness that was a challenge eagerly met by Charles and his growing sons.

Pioneer life changed boys into men almost overnight, and Watson Roe was no exception. At the advanced age of eighteen he married quiet, gentle-mannered Eleanor Platts, the daughter of a neighbor who had migrated from New Jersey. (A photograph of this prim little lady now hangs on the wall of my study together with a sampler that she made when she was nine years old. Her name, age and the year, 1811, are neatly embroidered with tiny, precise stitches.)

Grandfather was born in 1825, the second son of Watson and Eleanor. During the next thirteen years "Little Charles" with the red curls and blue eyes was the constant companion of "Big Charles" whose black hair was fast becoming well-sprinkled with white. While in looks small Charles did not resemble his grandfather, (both his mother and grandmother had auburn hair) he was much like his grandfather in both his ways and his abilities. They shared the same interests and instinctively seemed to share each others thoughts. More and more, as the years added up, the small grandson came to appreciate and to emulate his tall, energetic grandfather.

In August, 1838, tragedy struck with double force. Both Charles and Barsheba passed on suddenly within five days of each other. During their lifetime they had seen the United States grow from a narrow strip of states along the Atlantic Coast to a vast domain stretching as far west as the Rocky Mountains. They had lived through the stirring days of the Revolution and been a part of the great American Frontier, tilling ground that never before had felt a plow.

After their parents' death Watson, William and Eli sold their Indiana farms and continued the westward trek. In Michigan they again bought government land, this time in heavily forrested Berrien County where roads were mere paths through the woods. Because the land was purchased under arrangement effected by a treaty between Indians and the United States, the deed was approved and signed by the

President, Martin Van Buren, as well as the Secretary of War and the Commissioner for Indian Affairs.

In these "Big Woods" of Michigan where prowling wolves were still a menace Grandpa grew to manhood — the fourth generation to have a part in opening a way in the wilderness for the civilization that was to follow.

4

A NINETEENTH CENTURY IOWA FARM

"To the memory of all those pleasant, homely days of childhood when there was a wealth of resource that created what all the wealth of to-day does not — a reasonable content."

Della Lutes in *The Country Kitchen*

GRANDFATHER'S Michigan experience was invaluable after he arrived in Iowa where there were so many acres to clear of timber. Often he worked all day in the woods, cutting brush and splitting rails. One morning he awoke at dawn (or so he thought). He took his axe to the woods and began his day's work. When he finally realized that he had mistaken moonlight for daylight he was far too wide awake to think of going back to bed. By breakfast time, that morning, he had chopped and split one hundred rails!

During those early years in Iowa there was no railroad and the closest market for farm produce was Dubuque, a town on the Mississippi River fifty long miles away. It took Grandpa three days to make the trip — one day to go, one to sell his load and one for the return trip. When the new farmhouse was built in 1857 he hauled most of the lumber from Dubuque. The heavier timbers were hewn from trees that grew on the farm.

In this new country of northeastern Iowa where men made their own laws and abided by them, Grandfather's reputation for fair dealing won for him the respect of his neighbors and he was often called upon to settle disputes that arose. After carefully weighing the evidence he would talk to each man alone, and when he gave his opinion as to how the argument should be settled his decision was usually accepted as final for his judgment was considered fair and unbiased.

At one time a young couple in the neighborhood quarreled and the young woman sought asylum at the Roe farm. The next day Grandpa called on her husband and brought the young man home with him. After the "company supper" of fried chicken and strawberry shortcake (it was June) Grandpa, Grandma and the two guests retired to the parlor. The reconciliation effected behind tightly closed doors and tightly drawn blinds was highly successful and the young couple lived together "happily ever after."

Sarah Roe, like her husband, could be counted on for practical help in every neighborhood emergency. Even though she was a capable housekeeper and her home was the center of her interest, yet it was far from the circumference of her world and her activities. "To keep things going" Grandma often worked late into the night. Long after the family was in bed the

42

hum of her spinning wheel could be heard or the clatter of her loom. Farm homes were veritable factories in those early days. Grandpa took the wool to a mill to be carded, but from that point on Grandmother took over. Spinning, dyeing, weaving, knitting, (beside the more routine tasks of caring for the dairy, scouring, cleaning, baking and brewing) left very little leisure for the farm wife of a hundred years ago.

When the Civil War arrived, Grandmother was deprived of her two most valuable helpers. Eleanor and Mary, the two oldest daughters, were relegated to help their father keep the farm work going — a monumental task for one man and two young girls. The boys of the family were only curly headed youngsters at that time, and hired help was impossible to obtain. On the mornings when their father went to market, the girls were up at four o'clock to help load the wagon. After he left they took over the chores — the feeding of the stock and the milking.

The childhood of a hundred years ago did contain a generous portion of work, but there was fun as well. More often than not the good times were sandwiched into the work schedule. If a straw lot had to be cleaned up, there was always "time out" for picking a ripe watermelon and enjoying it in the shade of a big maple. When gooseberries or wild blackberries were ripe, there were excursions to the wild bushes that lined the paths through the pastures, and these trips were often the excuse for picnics. In a household of seven active children there was seldom a dull moment and often there was much good-natured teasing. Some of the family jokes of that day have been handed down through the years.

One story concerned Papa when he was a bashful boy of

fourteen. On a cold, wintry Sunday the family attended church as usual, and brought home with them a comely young lady who was to help with sewing during the coming week. Preparations were under way for Aunt Ett's wedding and the favored young man came home with them that day, too. Great Aunt and Great Uncle Torrey were also visiting at the farm and that evening the four guests, Grandpa, Grandma and Aunt Ett lingered around the fire in the dining room after the boys, George and Charles, had been sent to bed.

During the winter months the dining room served as a sitting room. The dining table was pushed back to make room for comfortable chairs that were pulled up close to the big "base burner." The boys' room was over the kitchen but the stair door leading to it opened out of the dining room. Their attic like room at the head of the stairs was so small that there was very little space between the stairs and the bed.

That night George was standing by the bed removing his undershirt when suddenly he felt his underdrawers drop down around his feet. With his arms pinned over his head and his eyes covered by his shirt he became confused as he attempted to free his feet. He squirmed and turned until, inadvertently, he stepped off into the stair well and was catapulted down the steep stairs!

At the landing, which led into the dining room, he turned a complete somersault and hit the door so forcibly with his feet that it flew open and poor George slid out into the room on his back — into the astonished presence of an attractive young lady, staid and proper Uncle and Aunt Torrey, his embarrassed sister, her beau and his mortified parents.

Gentle Grandma exclaimed, "Why George!" as she ran to cover him with her apron.

This stairway figured prominently in another adventure a few years later — the night George had his first date with a girl. On his return home, shoes in hand, he tiptoed to the stair door, hoping he would not disturb his sleeping parents whose bedroom opened off the dining room.

The stair door did not open with its usual ease and George was forced to give it a mighty tug. A string, holding the door from the other side snapped and, from the top of the stairs, there came a perfect avalanche of kitchen tinware! Everything from the wash-boiler to the dishpan tumbled down those steep stairs to welcome him home.

When quiet was restored there were muffled giggles from his sisters' bedrooms and his young brother, Charles, had disappeared to find a safer place to sleep than beside his more than slightly annoyed big brother.

Grandfather, like his Roe ancestors, was deeply religious. From the time of the Revolution when William Roe and his wife joined the church of which her uncle was pastor, the Roes were devoted adherents of the Baptist Church. All through the pioneer experiences of the family as they migrated to Kentucky, to Ohio, to Indiana and on into Michigan they opened their homes for church services until such a time as a meeting house could be built. While the Roes were living in Michigan a cousin of Grandfather's, another William Roe, became a minister in a denomination known as the "Christian Church." Such was his dedication to his faith that he soon converted the whole Roe family. Grandfather was an Elder in that church at

Arlington, a small town six miles away. He served there for over fifty years, from the time the church was organized.

Only once did Grandfather doubt the faith that he had adopted and that was of very short duration. In the early nineties Spiritualism became very popular around Strawberry Point. Strange tales were related by people whom my grandparents knew personally and considered reliable. After careful thought they decided to investigate this new doctrine for themselves, and the next time a seance was held they attended.

They were much impressed by the mysterious noises and communications which purported to come from those who had departed this world. But after returning home that night they were dismayed to find that the peculiar rappings they had heard at the seance had accompanied them home!

They endured the sepulchral sounds that seemed to issue from under their bed for quite some time. Then, after a whispered conference, they arose and, hand in hand, knelt by the side of the bed while Grandfather prayed for forgiveness. He promised God that neither he nor Grandmother would ever again try to solve the mysteries of the "spirit world." Such was their faith that they were not at all surprised when the queer noises ceased abruptly. And that night their sleep was sound.

Every Saturday night during Papa's childhood the family gathered around the kitchen table to study the Sunday School lesson for the following day. Seven little red heads and two older heads with hair of the same flaming hue (although somewhat dimmed by time) all bent together over their common task. It was at such moments that peace and contentment seemed to rest on the farm household like a benediction.

5

DAYS OF PLEASANT BREAD

"And the dear old Scotch Preacher, when Harriet and
I had wrapped him up, went out, saying:
'This has been a day of pleasant bread.' It has; it has.
I shall not soon forget it."

David Grayson, in *"Adventures in Friendship"*

THE HOSPITALITY of my grandparents was proverbial in northeastern Iowa where their farm was located. Travel was difficult and distances great a hundred years ago. The arrival of guests was considered ample reason for a gathering of the clan and sufficient cause for a celebration.

A letter written in 1865 by Great Aunt Myra tells of the cordial welcome that awaited her and her family at Grandfather's farm after their long, twenty-mile drive in the piercing cold of a January day. She describes in detail the bountiful table and the four happy families that gathered around it.

Not only were relatives and friends always welcome but "the

49

stranger within the gates" as well. During those early years (the state of Iowa was not five years old when Grandfather purchased the homestead rights of his large farm), many people were moving into that unsettled country. These immigrants often asked the privilege of camping on the "Common" — the elm shaded plot of ground carpeted with blue grass that lay between the fenced-in-dooryard and the road. No one was ever refused. Even friendly Indians were given a kindly welcome.

By the time the new century arrived, the children of this household were all established in homes of their own — all within a radius of ten miles of the home place. The reunions, then, took on added importance and were keenly anticipated by every member of this closely-knit group.

The family parties, traditionally, began early in the day and this custom was continued down the years. All of the men enjoyed hunting, and usually spent the morning of the reunion in the woods. In those days there was an abundance of rabbits, quail, partridge and squirrels for winter hunting, and prairie chickens were plentiful in the fall.

The women came equipped with aprons. They knew they would be expected to "help out" in the kitchen. In fact, the hours they spent together in the morning were perhaps the happiest of the whole day. It was then that they shared new "receets" as recipes were called, and it was then that the neighborhood news was recounted. Too, during the morning hours each woman had an opportunity to exhibit her culinary ability. It was: "Jessie, you make the chicken gravy, yours is as smooth as cream." Or, "Mary, your fillin' for 'punkin' pie is better than mine. When you make it today I'm goin' to watch how you spice it." Aunt Eleanor's buttermilk biscuits were justly famous, and no one could mash potatoes and achieve the miracle of mouth-watering goodness that Cousin Dory could. They were feathery light, snowy white, and smooth to the taste, with never a lump to mar their perfection.

What delectable and tantalizing smells issued from that huge, busy kitchen when a holiday dinner was in the process of preparation! Pies must be baked that very morning to be at their best, and there were always two kinds served at every winter party.

In the summer, there was at least one family party during the time that strawberries were ripe. Then dessert was sure to be strawberry shortcake. This tender, flaky cake (a very rich biscuit dough but *never* individual biscuits) was borne proudly to the table, heaped high with luscious fruit and oozing crimson juice from the warm, sweetened berries spread between the buttered layers. As Grandmother served us, we waited for Grandfather's time-honored remark: "Maybe God has made a better berry than a strawberry, but I've never tasted it."

The long dinner table was set in the "back-parlor" where the bay window was full of blossoming plants. With the beautiful tablecloth of hand-woven linen, the goldbanded china and the cranberry glass tumblers, the table, centered with its silver caster, was a breath-taking sight to a little girl.

After dinner was over the folding-doors to the front-parlor were thrown open and Mama took her place at the cabinet organ. Immediately the aunts and uncles joined her while the grown-up cousins made short work of the dishwashing task. Three of us who were considered too young to be of any help in the kitchen sat sedately on the horsehair sofa, seen but not heard, which was the law laid down for little children at the turn of the century. Grandma sat with us, but Grandfather usually joined the group at the organ.

Mama led the singing with her clear, true soprano well supported by Papa's booming bass. Two of the aunts had rich, contralto voices and several of the uncles sang tenor. Thus the parts were well balanced and the voices blended pleasantly.

The singing usually began with a ballad, a favorite of my father's and one they all loved to sing. The chorus had a gay, lilting melody which they sang with great gusto:

"Sailing, sailing over the bounding main,
For many a stormy wind shall blow ere Jack
comes home again."

Often this song was followed by the hymn that Grandma loved so well. She would nod her head in accompaniment as they sang more quietly:

"How gentle God's commands!
How kind His precepts are!"

As long as the singing continued we children were content to sit quietly and listen, but when the letter-reading and visiting began we usually slipped out to play — sometimes on the "Common," sometimes in Grandma's pleasant kitchen and often in the winter we tobogganed down the steep hill, across the road and out into the pasture.

One cold, winter Sunday (it was Aunt Ett's Wedding Anniversary) the singing had only started when big snowflakes began to sail past the frosted window panes. Usually we were not much concerned about the weather. If it was at all temperamental we stayed all night and that was added fun. But on this day Papa did not give the music his undivided attention but kept looking thoughtfully out the windows. A storm had been threatening all day and soon the wind began to sweep the snow in great gusts against the window panes. Papa stood up in sudden decision.

"I'm sorry to break up the party," he said, "but I don't want to get caught in a blizzard with Strawberry Point so many miles away.

There were cries of protest and Grandma said, "Can't you stay all night, George?"

Papa shook his head. "Being our town's only photographer has its drawbacks," he said. "I have an appointment in the morning to photograph a wedding party and must get home tonight."

Then all was sudden, bustling activity. Mama jumped up from the organ and ran to pack up. Grandma hurried to the kitchen to fix us a basket of food to carry home. Two of the aunts followed her to help and to wrap up our soapstone. (It had been heating in the oven of the kitchen range and would keep us toasty warm on the long ride.) Papa donned his ear muffs, fur coat and hat and left for the barn to harness Black Bess to the cutter, while Mama and I buttoned on our leggings and buckled up our overshoes. At Grandma's insistence we reinforced our coats with newspapers across our chests to keep out the bitter cold. Mama tied a fascinator over her hat and a heavy veil over her face, and I, too, wore a veil tied tightly over my "kitty" hood.

We were all bundled up and waiting when Papa drove up to

the door. As Grandfather carried me out to the sleigh, he slipped a small piece of horehound candy into my mittened hand with a knowing wink and a smile. Then, with a wave of hands and a jingle of sleigh bells we were on our way. The storm was at our backs and Black Bess, headed for home, stepped along willingly at a rapid pace.

As I snuggled down under the buffalo robe and thrust my hands into my muff, my fingers closed over the tiny piece of candy Grandfather had given me. Suddenly, deep down within me, I felt warm and secure as I thought of the family we had left behind us — the family so loving and beloved.

"Family parties are nice," I said with a contented sigh.

"Yes," Mama answered, as she pulled the robe tighter around us. "And these are the days we shall always remember."

How right she was! We shall not soon forget them — these days of " pleasant bread."

6

PARENTS ARE PEOPLE

THE KNOWLEDGE that parents are people came to me gradually as it does, I suppose, to most children. In a vague way I knew that both my parents must have lived before I arrived, but it was only as the little stories of their earlier experiences came to the surface that I began to appreciate them as individuals.

Papa, as the breadwinner, had many interests outside the home and he emerged a little faster as a person than did my mother. Too, I was regaled with fascinating tales of his childhood by his devoted, older sisters. But it was Mother who told me the story about Papa that I loved the very best. She referred to the incident many times during my growing-up years and it always made me very proud of my father but it never seemed to have that effect on Mama. And yet, through her eyes, I came to see how Papa faced untoward circumstances with equanimity and to appreciate how coolheaded he was in an emergency.

The summer that I was a year old the families — the Roes and the Hoags — vacationed at Lake Okoboji, a resort in northern Iowa. One late afternoon of a sultry day I was left with my maternal grandparents while Papa and Mama strolled down to the lake. The sky darkened as they stood on the shore and they saw storm clouds suddenly gather in the west. With a little anxiety they watched a boat idly drifting in the center of the lake. Little snatches of song were wafted to them on the breeze that was momentarily growing stronger, and they realized that the young couples in the boat were unaware of the clouds and their menace.

Suddenly the storm struck with demoniacal fury and the placid lake was instantly transformed into a churning ocean of towering waves. With horror my parents watched the little pleasure craft toss helplessly and then upend as though it were a fragile toy. Galvanizing into action, Papa commandeered a boat and, with a young lad to help him, was on his way to rescue the two couples who were clinging desperately to the overturned boat.

White-faced and frozen with terror, Mama stood in the wind and rain with the huddled group on the shore, straining to keep the rescue boat in sight as it rode wave after wave. When at last the rescuers reached the marooned young people and gently lifted them one by one to safety, a sigh of relief and a shout (quickly hushed) went up from the watchers on the shore.

Then again the tension as the dangerous return trip began. The small boat, loaded far beyond normal capacity, rode low in the water. Mama held her breath. What if the rescue boat should capsize! What possible chance would the two brave young men have with four exhausted people on their hands!

Finally, the harrowing suspense was over. The boat rode safely in on the crest of a wave and Papa and his brave companion were the heroes of the hour to everyone in camp — except one young wife. The strain on her had taken its toll. She maintained that there were others who should have volunteered who had less responsibilities and that Papa should have considered his obligations to her and me.

It was characteristic of Papa that he never tried to justify his action. I think Mama's attitude rather amused him, for he saw through her words to the fright she had sustained and the concern she had felt for his safety.

Perhaps because Mama was Mama and I could not believe that she could be happy without me, I didn't think of her often as an individual until I was almost grown.

My awakening came when I visited in a small Iowa town where an old-time friend of my mother's lived. When Dr. Toby was introduced to me he looked at me thoughtfully as he said, "So you are Ruby Hoag's daughter." It was the first time I had ever thought of my mother by her maiden name, and his words caught my attention. "Young lady," he continued, "did you know that your mother was a very beautiful girl?" Without waiting for an answer he spoke again, reminiscently. "She and her sister, Pearl, were known all through this part of Iowa as the two prettiest girls in the whole of Clayton County." Then, after looking at me intently for moment, he added, "You favor your father, don't you?"

I eagerly inspected the pictures Dr. Toby showed me of the pretty, brown-eyed young girl who was my mother and listened intently, almost unbelievingly, to the stories he told. He reminisced on and on about the parties, the picnics, the County Fairs, the dances on the sidewalk in the moonlight, and the boatrides on the river when they attended Teachers' Institute together. As he talked, I began to see my mother as I had never seen her before — as a person whose life was just as interesting as my own.

From that day forward my relationship with my mother changed. We were no longer just mother and daughter, but the best of friends, with mutual respect for each other as individuals. As the years piled up for me, they seemed to diminish for my Dresden doll mother, so that we were often taken for sisters — a fact that delighted my petite mother no end.

Recently a little box of mementos that my mother treasured came into my possession, and among her keepsakes I found an old letter that I had written to her in September 1949 when I was living in San Francisco. I opened the letter carefully, for it was badly frayed and worn from much reading. What could I have written that would mean so much to my mother, I wondered.

"Today was the first meeting since summer vacation of that study club I belong to," I read. "We were supposed to talk three minutes about the most interesting person we had been with during the summer, and can you guess whom I chose to talk about? Yes, YOU. Everyone was all primed to hear about some celebrity, knowing that Reynold and I had been on tour in the late spring." (My husband was a theatrical booking agent.) "Too, they knew that several famous people were in San Francisco this summer and that we had been with them. When I said, 'The most interesting person I visited with this summer was — my mother,' you should have seen the looks of astonishment on their faces!"

"I told them," I read on, "of the awakening I had years ago by that dentist friend of yours, and all the nice things he said about you. Do you remember? Then I told them how much fun we have had together down the years, how we spent our two precious weeks together this summer sorting over those huge boxes of old music and how, because of the memories they aroused of my childhood home, we couldn't destroy a single sheet but carefully tied them up again. Wasn't it fun singing and playing all those old favorites once more? I tried to make my friends see just what a marvelous childhood home I had, thanks to you and Papa."

As I replaced the faded letter in its box my thoughts turned again to that long ago day in San Francisco. I relived the misgivings that assailed me as the little cable car clanged its way to the top of Nob Hill carrying me to that meeting. What if my little talk fell flat! Three minutes to speak began to seem like an eternity. And then, that awful moment of dead silence when I finished speaking! Had I talked too sentimentally, too intimately, about my parents? Had I bored my friends? Perhaps

I had tried too hard to make them see that my parents were people — interesting people.

As I turned to the woman whose talk was to follow mine, she laughed shakily as she said, "Give me a moment to regain my voice and poise." Then, to my surprise, I saw others furtively wiping away tears, and I realized that as I had talked of my childhood home they had been reminded of their own; as I had described my parents they had thought of theirs — parents who were interesting individuals in their own rights.

The world over, parents are people, too. Very, very special people.

7

OVER PECK'S HARNESS SHOP

(Happy Childhood Days)

DURING the first five years of my childhood my father, mother, and I lived on Main Street in Strawberry Point, not far from the Four Corners and just across the street from the "Gallery," Papa's new photograph studio. For this three-room flat over Peck's Harness Shop my father paid the exorbitant rental of four dollars a month.

Probably I remember this item of the family finances because it has been referred to through the years as an example of the value of thrift.

"Keep your op'rating expenses *down* if you ever expect to get ahead," my father would say. And usually he would add,

"You don't make it until you *have it*," alluding of course to money. If Papa said he "made" a certain sum during a stated year, you knew without question that he meant there was that amount left over and above his living expenses. It was unthinkable for Papa to end a year just "breaking even."

Mama, on the other hand, although she believed as firmly as Papa that "a dollar saved is a dollar earned," sometimes liked to spend her "saved" dollar, not always in ways Papa approved of. One little extravagance of hers, for which I am grateful, was the collecting of souvenir spoons. I treasure them now, especially the one picturing my birthplace, Peck's Harness Shop, plainly etched on its gold bowl.

There is not too much that I remember about that first home, although the arrangement of the rooms and their hominess remain with me clearly. The steep stairs in the dark entrance hall led up to an entry room — another little hall at the rear of the building. An outside door there opened upon the rickety back steps, so steep and ladderlike that I was never allowed to negotiate them by myself. The backyard of the shop contained the well which supplied us with all the water we used. Great pailfuls had to be carried up those back stairs to supply the needs of the household.

Another door in the back entry opened directly into the kitchen and was the only entrance to the flat. This sunny, pleasant room ran the whole length of the building and its front windows faced directly on the street. Between these two windows stood our dining-table with the clock-shelf above it. Off the kitchen was a small room known as the pantry. What a well stocked room it was! In those days no one bought food in small quantities. Vegetables and fruits were sold by the peck or bushel, apples came in barrels, flour and sugar in hundred-pound sacks. My mother often traded piano lessons for farm produce, a fact that no doubt helped to keep our larder full to overflowing. Not only music lessons were exchanged for food but merchandise of every kind. We never spoke of going "shopping." We went "trading." And this was often literally true. Why bother with money when a dozen eggs could be traded at the store for anything from a spool of thread to a yard of calico?

Our parlor was used more than most parlors of its day, for my pretty little mother was the town's "music" teacher. Most of the lessons, especially those given to the children who came in from the country, were taught in our parlor. For these hour-long lessons Mama received a notable sum of twenty-five cents.

The most important piece of furniture in the parlor was, of course, Mama's well-loved and proudly owned up-right piano. Organs were quite common possessions at that time, but very few homes could boast of a piano. Beside it stood another luxury —a floor lamp which stood in all its dignity on three brass legs. Its brass bowl was kept well filled with kerosene and its flowered china shade was never guilty of dust or its glass chimney clouded with smoke.

Except for a square center table the rocking chairs (my own little one and two others) there was only one other piece of furniture in the parlor. It was an unusual combination of bookcase and desk. The bookcase with its long glass door protected Mama's music as well as our few books. The stereoscope with its pictures of Niagara Falls and The World's Fair was kept there, too. These pictures were mounted on little cards, each card showing two views of the same object. When the card was placed on the frame of the stereoscope and viewed through the eyeglasses of the instrument, the two pictures in some manner merged into one of great depth and clarity.

During musical evenings in our parlor, when friends of my parents dropped in for a "sing," I was allowed to sit, rock, and listen just as long as I could stay awake. The songs they sang were the popular ones of that day, such as "Love's Old Sweet Song" and "Annie Laurie." One that was quite a favorite during my childhood but wore itself out was, "Listen To The Mocking Bird." Another was a waltz song, "Only a Pansy Blossom," a favorite with my father. (No doubt due to the fact that it had been composed by a distant relative who had thereby amassed a tidy fortune.)

One song I remember, not for its music (I have no recollection of the tune) but for the unforgettable picture on the cover. The song was burdened by the sad and lengthy title, "She was Happy Till She Met You And the Fault Was All Your Own." The scene on the cover depicted a grim, middle-aged woman with arms akimbo standing in a doorway. Behind her a beautiful girl was weeping copious tears into her lacy handerchief, while a young man stood on the porch, facing the women with hat in hand and a pleading expression on his face. My sympathies, I remember, were all with the meek young man.

These evenings of music were even more delightful when gay Mr. Ocker was in town. He was a travelling salesman who possessed a tenor voice as strong as Papa's bass. How he

loved to sing — and eat popcorn. When he was due to arrive Mama built a hot fire, got out the old iron kettle, and popped a whole dishpan of fragrant, tender corn.

To pop corn in the days of the nineties was not the simple task of today. Corn did not come neatly packaged, shelled and ready to pop. Neither was it popped picturesquely over a grate fire in a wire popper. The ears of corn had to be shelled — a task not too easy for an amateur who attempted to loosen the tight, sharp kernels with his thumb. Papa was adept at this job and could rub one ear against another and accomplish the task in record time. The shelled corn must then be freed of its chaff. For that purpose it was placed in a shallow pan and carried outdoors. Mama usually took over at this point, for she was very particular to get rid of every husk. She would shake and blow, blow and shake until every kernel was clean.

In the meantime the heavy iron kettle was heating and the generous chunk of lard Mama had spooned into it was sizzling. The corn was stirred until the popping began. There was no need to shake the pot, even had that been possible, for never a kernel burned when it was popped in lard. Salt and butter were added after the popping was finished.

Juicy, red apples were considered the proper accompaniment for the popcorn, and for them the little gold-edged fruit plates were brought out and the little silver fruit knives.

In spite of my love for these "party" evenings I secretly felt they did not quite equal the afternoons when Mama played just for herself and for me. How beautiful to my ears were the long and rippling runs in Lange's "Flower Song," and the crashing chords in "The Johnstown Flood." But best of all was my own little song which came at nap time. "Go Tell Aunt Rhody," Mama would sing in her sweet, clear voice, and then the song grew softer and faded away, so that I never quite knew what happened to the "old gray goose."

The events of those first years spent over Peck's Harness Shop are hazy and sketchy, but one occasion I remember clearly — the day that Fannie, our faithful white horse, was turned out to pasture and Black Bess came to take her place. She was as spirited as Fannie had been gentle. How proudly Mama drove that bit of fire! They (Bess and Mama) were so much alike. Both were high-strung, both carried their heads high, and both were ladies of temperament. Perhaps that is why they understood each other so perfectly.

One day soon after the arrival of Black Bess Papa decided that our lively new horse needed a better bridle, and suddenly

I found myself (hanging tightly to Papa's hand) in the forbidden territory of the Harness Shop. I was seldom allowed to visit this intriguing place which enhanced my interest in it tremendously.

What a wonderful place it was! Sleighbells hung in gay festoons from a low ceiling. Buggy whips stood like tall sentinels in the dark corners of the room, and saddles and harness of every size and sort hung from pegs on the walls. And over it all was the good, clean, strong odor of new leather. While Papa and Mr. Peck conferred over the choice of a bridle, I made the most of this golden opportunity to look around. No telling when such a chance would come my way again.

Mama seldom ventured into this man's world. There was only one commodity in the shop that interested her particularly, and that she purchased early in the fall in a large enough quantity to last through the winter. Our quiet, reserved landlord was a true Vermonter and every fall he imported from his home state a goodly supply of maple syrup.

When a sign appeared in the shop window, "Maple Syrup for Sale," Mama was his first customer. It appeared on our table most often as a simple dessert — piping hot, buttered baking powder biscuits floating on an amber sea of slightly warmed maple syrup. What a treat on a cold winter night!

During the winter months road shows were often included in our weekly schedule. (Papa was the manager of the local Opera House as well as the town's photographer.) On those evenings I was allowed to spend the night with my maternal grandparents who lived a few short blocks away — an arrangement highly satisfactory with me. I heartily disliked the melodramas that were popular in that day. To agonize with the little girl who rescued her father from "Ten Nights In A Bar Room" was not my idea of a well spent evening.

In the late afternoon Grandpa Hoag would come for me and, with the snow creaking under the runners of my little red sled, we would journey up Main Street to the comfortable cottage where a doting grandmother and gay, teen-age aunts and uncles were looking forward to our arrival.

How pleasant to come from the chill and early dark of a winter night into the bright warmth of the cozy kitchen; to see, softly lighted by kerosene lamps, the long supper table ready and waiting for us. This is one of the many pleasant pictures memory has carried down the years of those happy days when we lived in the little flat over Peck's Harness Shop.

8

GRANDFATHER HOAG'S ANCESTRAL TREE

"All of good the past hath had
Remains to make our own time glad."

John Greenleaf Whittier

GRANDFATHER Hoag, my mother's father, was not quite forty-five years old when I was born, but with his snow white hair and long, white beard he was, to me, as ancient as the Ancient of Days. Never-the-less, during those years of my earliest childhood when my home was over Peck's Harness Shop, we were bosom companions for he was a champion story-teller. The true tales he told of his own childhood in Western New York State and the stories that were handed down to him of the wanderings and persecutions of his Quaker forebears were my favorites. These tales, together with the well-preserved Quaker records, have made the tracing of family history a fascinating and exciting adventure.

Almost two hundred years before Grandfather was born the immigrant ancestor, John Hoag, arrived from England. He was a weaver by trade and was known as a man of "good natural abilities." He located in the little town of Newbury, Massachusetts, and records show that he took an active part in the affairs of the village. One authority says he served at one time as a "side judge" until the magistrate began dealing mercilessly with the unfortunate people accused of witchcraft. John so vigorously opposed the prosecution of the victims that he was removed from office.

On April 21, 1669, he married a girl with the unusual given name of "Ebenezer." Her father, John Emery, had long been a respected citizen of Newbury. In 1641 he had been made a freeman, a coveted honor in the Colonies, and he held many important offices in the town.

Because of his standing in the community, John Emery felt that he might be able to sway public opinion on the side of justice in dealing with the persecuted Quakers, and he boldly entertained some Friends in his own home. But so strong was the prejudice against them that John was heavily fined. His petition for a remission of the fine was denied, even though it was signed by fifty citizens of Newbury as well as the town selectmen!

This experience was the beginning of the family's interest in the Quaker religion. Ebenezer was a girl of only fifteen when her father's hospitality to the Quakers resulted so unpleasantly, but by the time she and John Hoag were married — six years later — they both were ardent and active supporters of that faith. All of their children became devoted members of the

Society of Friends, and in a diary written by Judge Sewall of Newbury is found this interesting notation. Under the date of May 23, 1704, he wrote:

> "Went early to Salem conversed with Mr. Noyes, told him of the Quaker Meetings at Sam Sawyer's a week ago, the profaneness of the young Hoig's professing that heresy."

These "young Hoig's" were the sons of John and Ebenezer Hoag. Jonathan, the second son, was Grandfather's ancestor.

About a year before this incident recorded in Judge Sewall's diary, Jonathan had married Martha Goodwin, the daughter of a prominent Quaker of Amesbury. Jonathan and Martha reared their twelve children in Newbury, but in 1732 they left the comparative safety of the established communities of Massachusetts for a new settlement in the frontier state of New Hampshire. There they hoped to find more tolerance of their religion.

During the next forty years, like the Israelites of old, these dedicated Quakers wandered in a wilderness — a country wild and unsettled, constantly harassed by marauding Indians. Always motivated by the desire to find a home where they would be secure from religious persecution, they chose communities where Quakers had established themselves, but soon people of other faiths would settle nearby and the gentle Friends would again be subjected to the evils resulting from bigotry and malice.

The Hoags left New Hampshire in 1759 and settled on the east bank of the Hudson in New York State. By the time of the Revolution they were living near the little town of Easton. During the Burgoyne Campaign in 1777, the town was overrun by Hessians, Tories and, worst of all, Indians. The majority of the citizens fled to safer localities but the Hoags and some of their Quaker neighbors chose to stay and attempt to protect their property.

One Sunday they were gathered in the little Quaker Meeting House when a party of Indians — brutal looking savages with scalps dangling at their waists — burst in upon them. The Quakers never moved. With outward calm, though with beating hearts, they sat with heads bent in meditation and prayer. The warriors hesitated. These were the people who always treated them kindly; they were the ones who the bitter Red-Jacket said were the only white friends the Indians had. Impressed, too, by the quiet courage these gentle people manifested the red-men turned and silently withdrew.

About the turn of the next century, the Friends formed a new settlement in the wild, heavily forested region of Erie County in the far western corner of New York State. Jonathan Hoag's grandson joined the group in 1810 and bought a farm near Potter's Corners — a farm that stayed in the family for many generations. My great-grandfather, Alonzo Hoag, was born there in 1824.

Like his ancestors, Alonzo became a devout Quaker but he fell in love with a young woman whose family was as militant as his was peace-loving. The result was that he married "out of Meeting" and was "disowned" by the Society.

Emmeline Wheeler Hoag must have been well worth the sacrifice for she was a darling even in her seventies. She was a bouncy little woman of unlimited energy and interests. One of her talents, frowned upon by the Friends but adored by her great-grandchildren, was her ability to sing and accompany herself on a small accordion. Too, she loved to write jingly little verses and she bound them into books with our names inscribed on the covers in her own beautiful handwriting.

After their marriage Alonzo and Emmeline left the Quaker community to live for a few years at Cherry Creek in Chautauqua County. The summer of 1854 they returned to the farm for a visit and were there when Alonzo's father was bitten by a mad dog. My grandfather, Marion Alonzo, was only six years old at the time but he remembered the tragic incident only too well.

After his father passed on. Alonzo and his family remained at the farm. During the next eight years — those formative years for little Marion — he was educated in many of the Quaker ways of living. He often attended church with his grandmother in the quaint little Quaker Meeting House at Potter's Corners. The meeting always began in complete silence with no planned program of any kind, and the church was filled to overflowing with the somber garbed men, women and children. That Meeting House, built in 1810, still stands — a beautiful example of early American architecture with its hand-hewn beams and solid construction.

While these years on the farm were important for Marion and his two small brothers, it was an extremely trying time for their father. Alonzo was forced to live among his old friends but was no longer one of them, no longer one of the fold.

In 1862 Emmeline began to receive glowing letters from her adventurous brother who had migrated to the new state of Iowa. Perhaps the frowns of his one-time friends influenced

Alonzo to listen with favor to his wife's suggestion that he, too, move his family to this land of promise, for that very spring they made the long trip — via train and stage. A few weeks later they located in the small town of Strawberry Point.

Great-Grandfather, as I remember him, was an elderly man of seventy years. Tall, thin, with gray hair and long beard, he strode through my childhood in his faded, brown duster, a reserved, silent, lonely figure. His devotion to Great-Grandma and his pride in her was evidenced in ways that even a child could see, yet I have wondered if he did not miss the gentle companionship of those who believed and thought as he did.

9

A ROMANCE THAT BLOSSOMED
AT STRAWBERRY POINT

THE AUTUMN of 1867 — after Grandfather Hoag had taught school one year — an attractive young lady by the name of Luella Wolcott came to Strawberry Point to teach at a rural school not far from the one where he was in charge. Resourceful young Marion Alonzo found it comparatively easy to shorten recesses and dismiss his school a few moments early. He would then saunter over to Luella's school where, in his own words:

"He patiently sat under a tree so cool,
Waiting for her to let out school."

Grandfather loved to express himself in rhyme and many

years later he recounted in verse the story of his countship of Luella. His effort to do justice to the young lady's comeliness put rather a strain on the meter of the rhyme, but there can be no doubt as to his admiration of the young woman of his choice:

"No muse can furnish an adequate pen,
To fully describe her as she looked to me then.
She was lovely in form and in features fair,
Intellect bright as her brown eyes and hair."

Through several verses he goes on to tell of the good times they had together that winter of '67. The simple pleasures of that day — now a hundred years ago — seemed to center around the church and school. They attended church socials, box suppers, singing school, and even went square dancing, until they soon were an accepted "twosome" in Strawberry Point.

The smooth road to romance grew a bit rough when the young couple learned that Luella's parents had other plans for her. She began to receive letters from them urging her to return home to Wisconsin at the end of the school year. Luella obediently, although reluctantly, agreed to their wishes. Her decision, Marion Alonzo describes as a "real blow" to him.

There was no railroad into Strawberry Point at that time, and so, "in a rusty buckboard pulled by a balky pony" Marion Alonzo drove Luella along the dusty road to Elkader on the first lap of her trip back to Wisconsin. According to Grandfather, the long drive was made almost in silence for both of them were dreading the parting that was so imminent. Before Luella boarded the train, Marion Alonzo placed a "tiny ring on her hand as a small token of friendship."

The separation that summer proved too much for twenty-year-old Marion, and in his first letter to Luella went his formal proposal of marriage. She promptly replied (in the stilted language of the day), "I could ask no greater honor than to bear your name."

But the young couple's worries were not quite ended and Grandfather's verses indicate that the course of true love ran according to form. Luella's parents had "chosen a fellow for her to marry" with the promise to her that if she gave up the lad in far-away Iowa "the blame they would carry." Luella, however, in spite of her tiny stature (she stood on tiptoe to reach Grandfather's shoulder), had stronge courage and a mind to follow her own heart. She wrote to Marion Alonzo asking him to come to Wisconsin, saying, "I want my folks to see you and judge what I've done."

Sensing the importance of complying with her wishes, Marion immediately departed for the small village near Milwaukee. There he manfully faced inspection by the Wolcott family.

These relatives of Luella — her Grandfather Brownell and his son, as well as her parents — had pioneered in Wisconsin when that country was very new. Luella's father traced his family history not only through nine generations in the United States but fifteen generations more — back into the early history of England. The New England Wolcotts were prominent Puritans and one was well known in American history as a signer of the Declaration of Independence.

On the Brownell side of the family, Luella had three ancestors who arrived on the historic Mayflower; another married the daughter of John and Priscilla Alden whom Henry Wadsworth Longfellow immortalized; and still another had the distinction of being the grandaunt of President John Adams.

Luella's family soon recognized in the quiet young Iowan with his Quaker background the pioneer qualities and rich American heritage that their own family embodied, and willingly gave their consent to the marriage.

After a week of sight-seeing in and near Milwaukee the young couple left for Iowa, arriving at Elkader "in a hard August rain." They were welcomed back to Strawberry Point by Luella's married sister with whom she had lived the previous year. Luella's sister Lodema, who also was making plans to be married, joined her sister in Strawberry Point and together the two girls planned a double wedding.

"October twelfth, eighteen sixty-eight,
   Was the date set for the four to mate."

Grandfather had a new home ready for his bride soon after the wedding. The brown cottage built that fall on Main Street in Strawberry Point was home to them for over thirty years and their six children were born and reared there.

The romance of Marion Alonzo and Luella was a life-long one. The verses he wrote as a conclusion to the story of his courtship tell of his love that grew and mellowed with the years:

"Earthly gifts perish and vanish away,
   But the love for my Dear One will always stay."

The "Round Robin" letter that carried Grandfather's story to his children fifty years ago, still continues its flight to and fro across the country. Now it visits the grandchildren of Marion and Luella and occasionally pauses at the door of a newly established home of a great-grandchild. Then, Grandfather's verses are usually brought out and read to the new member of the family circle, and once more the romance that blossomed in Strawberry Point that eventful summer of 1868 blooms again.

10

COUSIN FRANCES AND
MY SECOND HOME

GRANDFATHER Hoag's brother, whom we called Uncle Eddy, his wife, Aunt Becky, and their three daughters lived at the west end of Main Street. I was delighted to find, when we moved up the hill to the Stearns Place in 1898, that our new home was almost directly across the street from theirs, and I was soon spending almost as much time there as I did at home.

Hospitable Aunt Becky had the happy faculty of making everyone in her home feel relaxed and comfortable. And she loved children, especially babies. Fretful ones would nestle in the security of her arms and in no time be fast asleep.

Aunt Becky's pride was her kitchen, her pantry and the long, long rows of canned fruits, vegetables and preserves in her cellar. She was never happier than when friends dropped in and she could share with them the fruit of her labors. Her cooky jar was never empty and her house always had the good smell of freshly baked bread, or Boston-Baked-Beans or maybe a cake just out of the oven.

While Aunt Becky was sociability personified, she was not interested in the slightest degree in the social whirl in Strawberry Point. Her chief worry was in satisfying her conscience that she had refused invitations without telling out-and-out fibs. I remember one time when her "regret" read that she had a previous engagement — and the "engagement" was a buggy ride into the country with Uncle Eddy.

Great-Uncle owned the drug store in our town and was a cheerful, kindly man whom everyone loved. With his rosy cheeks, merry, twinkling eyes and genial, friendly ways he appeared a veritable St. Nicholas to the small fry of Strawberry Point as, from behind the candy counter in his store, he dispensed corn candy and licorice sticks with a generous hand.

After the oldest daughter, Mildred, married, (I scattered rose petals at her large, church wedding) and the second daughter, Ida Mae, was away at school, I began to spend more and more time at this home across the street. By then, Mama was helping Papa at the studio and Ada, our capable hired girl, did not especially enjoy having her clean and orderly house mussed up by a little girl. Since Aunt Becky always made me welcome I soon formed the habit of going home from school with Frances, the youngest daughter of the household.

This young cousin of my mother's was three years older than I, yet when ages are eight and eleven, the bridge of years is not too difficult to cross. Besides, Frances had long been my ideal. I had endowed her with a name so fanciful that I guarded its origin carefully. "Fansy," I thought, sounds like Pansy and that is what she is — a beautiful pansy. Such a flight of fancy would have brought shouts of derisive laughter from the neighborhood — both from the young and old — this I had the good sense to know. Not even Frances herself knew why I had so named her, although she liked the name and in after years often used it when she signed her letters to me.

In spite of her quiet Quaker ways, this little girl with the round, flower-like face entered into the neighborhood games and charades with just as much zest as the rest of us. When we produced our neighborhood theatricals (which was as often as we could get the loan of a barn) it was Frances who, with utter lack of vanity, willingly took the more unprepossessing parts.

With curls tucked out of sight under an old cap, she would don a disreputable coat of her father's and strut about the stage burnt cork beetle-brows and homemade beard masking her features effectively. I can see her yet as the villain in one of our top productions. With extreme braggadocio, she brandished her toy pistol as she declaimed in tones of disdain, "This is no gun — it's a son-of-a-gun," a daringly risque speech (considered the height of humor) and one which rolled our young audience (six pins admission) in the aisles and brought down the house.

Aunt Becky was good-natured and never seemed to mind

the paper dolls that littered the house. In fact, she saved for us all her old "Delineators" whose fashion plates (we thought) made beautiful dolls. She enjoyed all our fun and often entered into our play. On rainy days we could count on her cooperation to help us create new wardrobes for our china-headed babies (she was an expert with a needle) and, if it chanced to be baking day, we were allowed to roll out our own gingerbread men and frost our own cookies.

While Aunt Becky was most tolerant of the clutter that came with little girls at play, she had a wholesome dislike for both dirt and sloth. Both of these undesirable qualities were personified in the town's professional loafer and gossip. Tim was a shoemaker but only worked at his trade when hunger drove him to it. From morning until night he held forth on a drygoods box wherever he could find a small knot of men to listen to him orate. Dirty, ill-kept, with a matted beard and uncombed hair he was a disreputable figure.

The only time that Tim was ever known to lack for words was in an encounter one morning with Aunt Becky. He had been soaking leather over night and he chose to empty the huge tub of black water out the door of his shop just as Aunt Becky was passing by. She stepped back quickly to avoid the onslaught and her disgust of the man and his lazy, slip-shod ways rose up within her as she watched the dirty-looking river ooze through the cracks of the board sidewalk.

"Well, Tim," she said sweetly, "I'm glad to see you've had a bath." Then, with raised skirts she picked her way daintily across the wet sidewalk leaving Tim speechless in his doorway.

Friday nights I had a standing invitation to stay for supper.

Afterwards there were games — Dominoes, Flinch or Authors — and sometimes Uncle Ed would play his cello. This jolly uncle could bring forth from the deep-toned instrument gay, lively tunes that were pure delight or, when in sober mood, strains that sobbed with emotion and were rich and beautiful. I have no remembrance of anyone ever accompanying him, although there was a big, rosewood square piano in the bay window of the parlor. Often I would play on it something I had practiced and learned during the previous week. And I was always sure of a loving and appreciative audience.

When Frances entered High School I was only ten and, though our ways began to separate, strangely enough the bond between us grew stronger. It was then that I began to look to her for sisterly counsel. Aunt Becky continued to include me in the family circle, and this substantial home remained my second home all the years we lived in Strawberry Point.

11

THE SMALL WORLD OF YESTERDAY'S CHILDHOOD

STRAWBERRY Point was my universe back in 1898, and the whole World centered in our yard. Our large, rambling, two-story house stood well back from the street and was located on the corner of Main Street and Maxim's Lane. The side yard was large enough to accommodate all the children in the neighborhood, and they were usually there during the long, summer twilights.

Often we would play games until nine o'clock at night — games of Pom-Pom-Pull-Away, Run-Sheep-Run, Blind Man's-Buff, Hide-And-Seek or Statue. Another favorite was a game that entailed an ability for pantomime. In our Iowa town we called it "Lemonade." Under various names children have played this game for generations, and probably still do although the side yards of the nation have retired in favor of supervised playgrounds. In our particular version, after choosing sides and going into a huddle to decide our "trade," we of the visiting team went toward our opponents and the patter that ensued as we neared the "enemy" base went something like this:

"Here we come."
"Where from?"
"New Or*leans*."
"What's your trade?"
"Lemonade."
"Show us some."

With that, we of the visiting group would industriously ply our trade with realistic gestures and facial expressions until some bright member of the opposing team guessed our secret. When he shouted his discovery loud and triumphantly we flew for "home base," for those who were caught must suffer the ignominious fate of being forced to join the enemy ranks. What breathless excitement! What fun!

When for some reason we were few in number, or it was too hot a night for strenuous games, we would stamp white horses as we swung idly in the hammock or stretched out on the lawn. As soon as a white horse would come into view — far down the street — a tongue-dampened thumb would be quickly pressed to the palm of the other hand, and a quick fist would stamp the moistened spot, energetically registering the arrival, or rather the departure, of one more white horse.

Sometimes we would leave our play to follow old Mr. Dalton

as he went about lighting the street lamps — small kerosene
lanterns set on high posts. The preliminary work to lighting the
lamps Mr. Dalton took care of earlier in the day — filling the
lamp-bowls with oil, trimming the wicks and cleaning the
smoky film from the glass windows of the lanterns. At nightfall
he would begin his journey up and down Main Street, a small
stool clutched in one gnarled hand, a box of matches in the
other. At each lamp-post he would climb on his stool and lift
a lighted match to the wick of the lantern. When the flame
caught, he would close the little door of the lamp, pick up his
stool and trudge patiently on his way. The quiet of his measured
tread was broken only by the soft *plop, plop* of small bare feet
on the board sidewalk as his admiring audience trotted after
him — a respectful distance in the rear. Our friendly lamp-
lighter (he was also the school janitor) always seemed glad
of our company if we did not bother him in his work. We
children considered him one of our best friends and he knew
each one of us by name.

It was on my sixth birthday that the side yard became the
setting of my first party. The dining table had been brought out
into the yard for the occasion and stretched to its full length
for the celebration. Mama used her very best tablecolth with
the large "R" embroidered on it, and with the two tall cake
plates of fluted milk glass and the pretty flowered Haviland
china, the tea-table was an impressive sight. Each little guest,
as she arrived with her doll, felt impelled to don her very best
company manners. It was only at such "formal" functions that
we condescended to allow our play to be supervised or guided
by adults. Ordinarily we would have felt embarrassed and re-

stricted if grown-ups had so entered our childhood world. But parties were different. There we obediently and decorously played the games suggested — quiet, lady-like games such as "Drop-the-Handkerchief," "London Bridge" and "I Spy" (the later known in some circles as "Hide The Thimble.")

One night, I remember, our side yard was taken over by grown-ups as well as children. A cousin of Papa's, Harry Roe, who lived in Manchester, another small town twenty miles away, had organized a Mandolin Club, and he brought the group to our home one warm summer evening. These young men, using our side porch as a stage, played and sang for us the many popular songs and ballads of that day. After a little urging (not much was needed) Papa joined them with his guitar. Soon the crowd began to gather and suddenly it seemed the whole town was there, sitting on our side lawn. How the young voices harmonized in "Annie Laurie," "In The Gloaming," and "Sweet Genevieve." They rose clear and true on the still, night air, carried and supported by the tinkling strings of twenty mandolins and the deep, strong rhythm of the lone guitar.

One summer day our side yard had an unusual and not too welcome visitor. Gypsies often camped just outside our town and would come in to beg or steal whatever struck their fancy. Mama was afraid of them, I knew, and there were sorry tales whispered around of little folk being kidnapped and carried away by these irresponsible people. Their flashy dress and their unconventional way of living as well as the stories told of them made us wary and we kept well out of their way when they made a camp near our town.

On this particular day, as I sat at the piano practicing, my attention was attracted by a noise at the open window that overlooked our side yard and Maxim's Lane. I glanced up from the music — and instantly froze to the piano stool. There, not an arm's length from where I was sitting, stood a grinning, young gypsy, her feet firmly planted in Mama's lilies-of-the-valley. Her face was close to the window screen and her large, brassy earrings were shaking back and forth as she bobbed her head in time to the music.

When my practice stopped abruptly, Mama, who was in the next room, stepped to the door and, at sight of our visitor, she, too, became transfixed and speechless. But when she saw the havoc that had been wrought in her precious flower-bed she regained her voice speedily and with unmistakable firmness she ordered the woman out of the yard. The gypsy laughed, shrugged her shoulders and tripped off down Maxim's Lane. And Mama and I were left with the rather uncomfortable impression that the gay, care-free young vagabond had, if anything, less respect for our way of living that we had for hers!

Summertime in the side yard was not all fun, but the work-a-day world entered gently and quietly without pressure or urgency. Very often on summer mornings Mama and I would take our tasks to the shady side porch and there shuck peas or string beans as we swung in the hammock. My dolls gained new wardrobes on that same side porch as I learned to hold a needle and take tiny, running stitches. As we worked, we talked. And I learned. I went to school every summer to my mother and never knew I was there. Children at the turn of the century had few professional teachers but acquired their skills in everything from sewing to swimming by example as well as precept. To have been a child in that leisurely, unregimented world of yesterday was a privilege, especially in a small Iowa town like Strawberry Point, and in a home with a yard like the one at the corner of Main Street and Maxim's Lane.

12

THE ARRIVAL OF THE
NEW CENTURY

WHEN New Year's Day, 1900, was due to arrive there was much talk in Strawberry Point of the "New Century." Just what was meant by that term I did not exactly understand. A big New Year's Eve party had been planned to celebrate the occasion, that I knew, and it was to be held at "Man" and "Lady" Steele's. When these good friends dropped in for an evening of music, I was allowed to share in the fun, but this occasion (it had been explained to me) was different. This was to be definitely a grown-up party and no children were invited. Finally the decision was reached that I should be put to bed that night in Norma's room. Norma, the grown-up daughter of the Steele's, was to be out that evening, celebrating with her own friends.

With Mama, excitement ran high the day of the party. She had a new blouse for the affair, made by the town's most expensive dressmaker. It was a beautiful, plaid silk trimmed with tiny black velvet ribbon bows and made in the latest fashion with a high boned collar and "leg-o'-mutton" sleeves. With it she planned to wear her long, black taffeta skirt with the ruffled flounce that swept the floor. It made a stunning outfit and she was very pleased with it.

The party seemed to react quite differently on Papa. Perhaps Mama's extravagance (the blouse had cost an outrageous sum for that day) subdued him somewhat. That night at supper he became quite philosophical.

"Here we are," he said, "planning to attend a silly 'Watch Party,' eat chicken salad and mince pie at midnight, and giving no thought whatever to the seriousness of the hour."

"What is so serious about it?" Mama questioned blithely. She was in excellent spirits. (The blouse fitted perfectly.)

"This is no ordinary New Year's Eve," Papa replied. "Don't you realize that tomorrow is the beginning of a new century? We are in the midst of a changing world. A good many believe that our country is on the brink of departing from its policy of isolation in world affairs. If it does, that may affect all our lives."

Mama was a bit sobered by Papa's earnestness and asked quietly, "What makes you think that we are about to mix into European affairs?"

"Because ever since our war with Spain year before last, the attitude of the world toward us has changed. All nations hold us in respect now. The papers have been full of the difference of our position in international affairs. We are now the sponsors for law and order in Cuba. No country is going to forget that."

"Well, I am glad that taking the little island under our wing has accomplished so much, but I really don't like the prospect of a change in our way of living," Mama said. "I like things the way they are."

Papa laughed. "You can't stop the wheels of progress when they get to rolling. Science and invention are fast coming into their own. There is a man in the Far East who already has done marvelous things with electricity. The telephone will arrive in our town any day now, and horseless carriages are bound to come. Why, during our lifetime we may even see men fly."

During this conversation I had been a wide-eyed listener. Now I could contain myself no longer.

"Papa, if men fly will they have wings?" I asked breathlessly.

Papa smiled. "I hardly think so," he said. "Although one man did try it. He made huge wings and attempted to use them like a bird. Another man I read about built a ship that he tried to fly like a kite, but that didn't work either. No one knows whether air travel will ever be practical. Time will tell."

"I wouldn't mind having a few inventions to simplify housework," Mama said with an indulgent smile. "A new kind of broom, perhaps, that would pick up the dirt as well as sweep it." and she laughed merrily at her own ridiculous idea.

But Papa did not laugh. "It's possible," he said stoutly. "There are bound to be many conveniences invented during this coming century. In Cedar Rapids, I understand, many of the better new homes already have bathrooms."

"If we could have a bathroom like your folks have, that would be real nice," Mama said thoughtfully. "But I don't believe that I would want one in the *house*."

Two years before, Grandfather Roe had added a room to the rear of his house that had caused plenty of comment. It was connected to the rest of the house by a high cement platform or porch, and it was dependent for heat upon a small kerosene stove. The only fixture in the room was a huge built-in bathtub made of galvanized iron. The tub was filled with water drawn from the well just outside the door and heated in the nearby kitchen — an arrangement considered a great convenience in 1898. The bath water was piped out from under the tub and this in itself was considered an unusual achievement. I myself had enjoyed the luxurious treat of a bath at Grandfather's house, and watched with fascination the water gurgle down the drain. I hoped fervently that the new century would supply us with such a delightful convenience.

"During the coming century I'll wager there will be big changes in my business, too," Papa said. "A photographer at Kansas City who gave a talk to us at the last convention said that within thirty-five years we might be able to photograph color. Imagine that!"

"I imagine we'll be late to the party if we don't stop talking," Mama said as she rose from the table. "I want to get there a few minutes early so as to get Flossie to bed before people come."

Privately, I didn't think much of the idea of being put to

bed when so much was going on. I wanted very much to be on hand when the 1800's changed to 1900. I, being six-going-on-seven wasn't sure what was going to happen, but I intended to stay awake just the same.

At my request Mama left the bedroom door ajar and for awhile I lay contentedly listening to the laughter and the music that floated up to me from below, while thoughts of airships, horseless carriages, bathtubs, and telephones flitted idly through my mind. It was pleasant in the little room with its white-painted furniture and snowy white ruffled curtains — pleasant to listen to the happy chatter in the rooms downstairs. And then — despite my firm resolution, I drifted off to sleep. When I awoke the next morning, I found to my keen disappointment that the much heralded celebration was over. So far as I was concerned, the arrival of the New Century was entirely over-rated!

13

SPRING CLEANING HAS COMPENSATIONS

HOUSE CLEANING week was an ordeal that our family faced each spring with mixed emotions. On the plus side of the ledger was the fact that it usually brought an invitation from Aunt Alma to have dinner with her the Sunday after the house was put in order. A dinner at Aunt Alma's was always an event, especially when Cousin Dory presided in the kitchen, but it took on added attraction the week of spring cleaning when meals at our house were meager and sketchy.

This week of weeks, too, always heralded the fact that Iowa's warm weather had definitely arrived and that at last I would be allowed to discard my heavy, long woolen underwear. For weeks before the event I would beg, "Isn't this the week I change?" But Mama was cautious and had to be real sure that the weather was "settled" before the stoves were removed and the house made ready for summer living.

When I would come skipping up Maxim's Lane from school to find the carpets on the clothes line, the carpet beater in action, the mattresses spread out on the lawn and general confusion in the house, then I would know that "The Day" had arrived. Now my little ruffled panties and cotton panty-waist would be allowed to take the place of the hot, long woolens that reached to and were tucked into the tops of my shoes. What a relief that change was! It almost made up for the confusion downstairs — almost but not quite. Mama was a termigant that week of turmoil and wielded her broom with a high hand.

To Papa and me, spring house-cleaning meant a world turned topsy-turvy; but to Mama, I really believe it was an orderly procedure. She was a general who planned her campaign weeks in advance and in her mind's eye she saw only the victory that was bound to follow her organized battle against dust and dirt. The exact date of the attack was settled by the Weather Man, yet when it arrived she was ready. Hired help had been arranged for and the whole household was immediately mobilized with the one exception of Papa. By supplying and paying for the extra help, he felt that he had provided an adequate substitute for himself. His business at the photograph gallery always seemed especially heavy on that week of household activity, but he didn't escape being drafted for special jobs.

With an apron belting down her old "Mother Hubbard,"

her hair enveloped in a dust cap or kitchen towel, Mama directed her campaign. Every bed had to be taken apart and every section thoroughly cleaned, storm windows replaced with screens (Papa's responsibility), walls wiped down and some rooms repapered, the carpets taken up (the good tacks must be saved to be used again) and the floors swept and scrubbed. Papa strung an extra clothes line between the blossoming apple trees and reinforced it with forked poles, for not only were room size carpets hung out but every comforter and blanket as well. The windows, shining with an extra polish, exuded the strong, prickly smell of ammonia.

Last of all came the laundering of the delicate lace curtains with their elaborate borders. This task was accomplished under Mama's personal supervision for the fragile lace had to be stretched carefully on narrow curtain frames while the material was still damp. When they were dry, the curtains were ready for the windows and no flatiron could possibly improve their starchy primness.

With the cleaning finished, the beds fresh and sweet-smelling from their day's sojourn in the sunshine, the well-beaten carpets laid over fresh straw and tacked securely to the floor with the aid of a carpet-stretcher, and the crisp curtains all hung at the sparkling windows, then Mama rested on her laurels. The whole effort, even to Papa and me, did seem worthwhile.

The spring of 1900, housecleaning had been especially thorough. Mama had been unusually painstaking, spurred on by the prospect of a new rag carpet for our parlor. All winter long we had worked, preparing mountains of rags. The material, torn into inch wide strips, was sewed end to end. The work of winding them into balls was mine. (A penny a pound was the going price for this job.) Mama's carpet that year was especially pretty, for she had dyed all of her white cottons blue. Although it was woven "hit-or-miss" on a wide loom by old Mrs. Woodruff, the one color predominated and made the whole carpet look (as we thought) almost "store made."

Mrs. Woodruff had learned her trade when a girl in England. Her loom sat like a huge organ in a corner of her parlor, and she sat before it like the artist that she was. No organist at her console ever brought forth harmonies or blended her tones with a surer touch. At her left stood a clothes basket filled to overflowing with the colored balls of wound carpet rags. How I loved to stand beside her as she worked — to hear the clatter of the loom and watch the colors change as the shuttles shifted from side to side.

One day soon after the house was put in order and the new carpet in place, Mrs. Woodruff dropped by to view the result of her handiwork. As she looked around at the spotless, shining house she shook her head in smiling disapproval.

"You keep your 'ouse too clean, Miz Roe," she said. "A little dirt is 'ealthy. You're much too pa'ticular with your 'ouse-cleaning."

Mama laughed. "Yes," she said, "I suppose I am. Thorough house-cleaning is a lot of work, but I think it has its compensations."

Compensations! This long word was a new one to me and I said it over and over to myself. I had no idea what it meant so after Mrs. Woodruff left I questioned Mama.

"Compensations are sort of a reward," she said. "When

you work hard in school and are rewarded by a good grade, that is compensation for your work."

Just what the reward of house-cleaning week was I couldn't possibly imagine, but I didn't say so. I had added a new word to my limited vocabulary and that satisfied me for the moment.

Spring cleaning that year brought the usual welcome invitation from Aunt Alma and the information that Dory would be on hand to cook us a chicken dinner. Sunday noon found us attired in our very best clothes. Mama was again her stylish self with a pretty flowered leghorn hat atop her dark hair. Papa, with his long mustache twirled just so, looked very handsome as he bowed and lifted his new straw hat to all the ladies we met on our way down town. I wore a cool, pink dimity dress and now there were no heavy woolens under my long, black stockings.

As we walked along Strawberry Point's quiet Main Street on our way to Aunt Alma's, visions of the coming feast floated before my eyes. Suddenly I thought of my new word and knew how to use it. No heavy woolens; A chicken dinner! Of course, Spring House Cleaning Week did have its compensations!

14

WHEN MAMA BROKE WITH TRADITION

VERY soon after I was eight years old, Father opened two branch photograph galleries and was in real need of an assistant. After several months of a steady procession of agency supplied "help" who were both irresponsible and inefficient, Mama saw opportunity walking her way.

There was much drudgery connected with household tasks in those years at the turn of the century, even in town homes and in households as small as ours, so it is not surprising that Mama with her keen mind was eager for a change. Today we are inclined to take laundries, dry-cleaning establishments, bakeries, and even beauty parlors very much for granted, but in the early 1900's all these services were performed under the home roof.

There was not even a hand-operated washing machine in our small Iowa town, and all ironing was accomplished with what were known as sadirons — and they were well named. These big, heavy irons were heated on the woodburning kitchen range, and the heat made the task of ironing all the numerous and lengthy petticoats that were popular in that day even more tiresome and distasteful.

There were no commercially canned foods then, at least in our home. All summer long Mama canned — sometimes fruits, sometimes vegetables, sometimes meats. (Even stewed chickens were "put up.") She made jellies and preserves, pickled cucumbers and peaches. Then there were quarts and quarts of milk to be taken care of, for like most small-town families, we kept a cow. Having all the butter we wanted to use we accepted as our natural right. No cakes or cookies at our house were ever shortened with anything less than real butter. When Mama baked bread, which was twice a week, how good the fresh crust tasted (we called it the heel) spread generously with butter fresh from the churn!

As to beauty parlors, Mama came closer to this extravagance than most women of her day. Since her beautiful, almost-black hair was thick, long, and difficult for her to handle, Leslie Chase, the town barber, came to our house to shampoo it. Sometimes Mama would sit out in the sunshine while her hair dried, but usually Leslie would fan it dry, using a large, palm-leaf fan.

"Duty" was a word my mother always spelled with a capital

letter. I am sure that she would never have voluntarily left her home for a career if she had not felt that Father's predicament in not being able to get competent help in his growing business justified her radical step. As it was, she had no easy task when she attempted to sell him on the idea.

In those days women did not leave their homes for other work, no matter how interesting it promised to be, not unless there was a dire need. But at last Papa was won over. The day came — the tragic day for me — when Mama was no longer at home to see me off for school or to welcome me home at night. A hired girl was installed at home and Mama entered into her new job with schoolgirl enthusiasm.

After Mama began to work at the studio, it was always doubly hard to get off to school on time. One morning I was especially slow. Ada, the hired girl, said I dawdled and, no doubt, I did. Anyway, I suddenly realized that, even running "cross-lots" down Maxim's Lane and across the pastures, I could never get to school on time. To be tardy was a terrible disgrace and considered far worse than just being absent from school, for when that happened there were usually extenuating circumstances. My only hope, I realized, was to prevail upon Mama to let me stay at home that day. With lagging steps, I took the Main Street road and climbed the stairs to the gallery.

Tears were flowing and I was prepared for Mama's sympathetic cooperation. Surely she wouldn't make me go to school and be *late*! I was never more mistaken. Mama took one look at my tear-stained face and without waiting for any explanations she grabbed me by the hand.

I was running to keep up with her by the time we reached

the Four Corners and started down South Street. Just as we were passing Appleby's Grocery Store, Claire Treadwell, the good-natured lad who delivered groceries, came out of the store and climbed unto the delivery wagon. Then Mama had an inspiration.

"Claire," she called, "will you take my girl to school?" Then, as an afterthought, "Do you suppose you could get her there on time?"

"Sure thing, Ruby," he replied, answering both questions. "Hop in, Flossie, and let's go."

I needed no further invitation. In no time I had climbed over the wagon wheel and pulled myself up onto the high seat of the spring wagon.

Startled at the unaccustomed touch of the whip, old Skip, who usually travelled a very leisurely pace, broke into a run. Hanging onto my precarious perch as we bounded over the rutty road, I began to have a glimmer of hope. Just maybe we would make it, if only kind Mr. Dalton, the school janitor, saw us in time.

Even before we came in sight of the school we heard the last bell, but we knew that Mr. Dalton, sitting in his cupola window, would be on the lookout for stragglers. Claire waved his whip to attract attention to us and our friendly janitor returned the greeting with a wave of his hand. The bell rang on and on as I climbed out of the wagon and sped up the school walk.

Without stopping in the cloak room, I rushed into the schoolroom and stood safely inside the door when the bell gave forth its final peal. Panting, with a flushed, tear-stained face, my hat hanging on the back of my head by the rubber under my chin, I must have presented a sorry picture. But there was no tardy mark to stain a perfect record.

When Mama courageously broke with tradition and proved to her friends and neighbors that "Woman's Sphere" could successfully include a career outside the home, she did not immediately convince me.

One morning, a few weeks after the wild ride to school on the grocery truck, I awakened feeling anything but myself; and this time I had no trouble gaining permission to stay home from school. I have never forgotten the desolate feeling of loneliness that engulfed me as Mama left for work. I stood at the window with my face pressed close to the glass to watch her until she was completely out of sight.

By night I was delirious and the bout with Death was on. For weeks the battle waged while my life hung on the proverbial thread. That I came forth the victor was due, according to the family physician, to my mother's prayers. "The child's recovery was a modern miracle," he said.

The day I returned to consciousness, the whole world seemed shiny and new. The spare bed had been moved down to the parlor and there I lay, day after day, perfectly content as I watched Mama who, career forgotten, went quietly about her home, helping Ada with the household tasks.

There was no more school for me that year and all through the lovely warm days of May and June I was allowed to run and play, to gather wild flowers in the pastures and gain back my strength in the freedom of the fields and the countryside.

My illness, although it slowed up Mama's career, did not

discourage her. By summer she had returned to the studio, but my school books and I went along. She devoted part of every morning to coaching me on the school work that I had missed. While she developed plates or retouched negatives, I recited the multiplication table and spelled pages of words. By September I was well able to take my place with my class without any sense of strain.

That summer I made the important discovery that Mama's career was of no great consequence after all, that it would never be allowed to interfere with home interests. From that time on, I accepted the changes in our home with very good grace. The "tragic day" gave way to the "magic day" when the realization dawned that Mama was Mama whether she was at home baking bread or at the gallery printing pictures. For all practical purposes, the gallery became Home. I reported there after school every afternoon and then went happily out to play.

15

GRANDMOTHER'S MANTLE

THE DAY before Grandmother Roe left us, she asked to
see me. Why of all her eighteen grandchildren I was the
chosen one, we did not know. Probably because I was the
youngest of the lot and she was concerned about my spiritual
welfare. Papa was the only one of her children who had not
joined the church. He and Mama were considered worldly in
those days for they loved to dance and play cards, two activities
frowned upon by almost every denomination.

Whatever the reason, Grandma's wish was not to be ignored,
although Mama was not too pleased with the request. I am sure
that she feared it might be an ordeal for an impressionable child.

I was prepared for the visit by my anxious aunts. I was not to speak to Grandma unless she questioned me. I was to be very quiet and leave promptly when Grandma dismissed me. I entered the familiar room on tiptoe and stood quietly by the bedside. Grandma attempted a smile as she placed her hand on my curls. She spoke with great difficulty — perhaps that is the reason her few words impressed themselves so vividly on my memory. "Flossie," she said and her words came very slowly, "always be a good girl." Then I was lifted up to kiss her and someone led me away.

For many years I never spoke to anyone about that visit, but I thought about it a great deal. Grandma had put her hand on my head just as the patriarchs of Bible times had done when blessing their sons. There was a picture in my book of Bible stories showing Isaac blessing Jacob by putting a hand on his head. Had Grandma blessed me too? I wondered and pondered over it often when I was alone. Certainly she had told me what to do. I read into her simple words a solemn command.

Grandmother's funeral was held in the little church in Arlington where she and Grandfather had been so active for many years. It was a ten-mile drive from there to the Strawberry Point Cemetery, and the fact that there were over a hundred carriages in that long procession made a great impression on me — a child of nine years. This slow moving cavalcade of sympathetic friends made me realize, probably better than any eulogy could have, the love and esteem my grandparents had earned in the community.

Years later, when I was a young woman, Papa and I were

sitting on the porch one summer evening talking, as we often did, of his wonderful family. Then, for the first time I told him how impressed I had been by that last visit to Grandma. How, all through the years, I had felt that, in a way, Grandma's mantle of human goodness had been dropped upon my undeserving shoulders. I talked haltingly, for even from the pinacle of adulthood I continued to feel the responsibility of living up to Grandma's wishes.

For a few moments we sat silent, listening to the night sounds and watching the flicker of the fireflies on the lawn. Papa's voice was not too steady when he finally offered his comment. "If you are half as good a woman as your grandmother," he said huskily, "you'll do all right."

16

THE NEW HOUSE
ON MAIN STREET

THE WINTER of 1903 our family's interest centered on the building of a new house. Every evening, after the supper table was cleared and the dishes done, Mama would pull down the hanging lamp over the dining table and she and Papa would pore over the plans and blue prints spread out before them. Architects were unheard of in Strawberry Point, and I don't remember that any consideration was given as to how the house would *look*. All attention was centered upon the size and arrangement of rooms.

Papa had purchased a lot on Main Street only a block from the business district. Mama thought it would be more convenient to live close to the photograph gallery since she expected to continue working there. The lot was in a good neighborhood, even though it was near the center of town. Doctor Eaton, the town's dentist, had just finished building a new house on the lot next to ours, and directly across the street was the large, lovely new home of dignified Senator Newberry. The Methodist Church and parsonage were also in our block. This I considered a big advantage, for Clara DePuy, the minister's daughter, was my bosom companion. (The winter her father read aloud "The Little Shepherd of Kingdom Come" — one chapter was read each morning after Family Worship — I joined the DePuys regularly for morning prayers.)

In planning the New House, the "Wants" and "Needs" were of primary consideration. I had always been taught that there was plenty of money for "Needs" but very little for "Wants." Heretofore the line had been so sharply drawn that it had never occurred to me that "Wants" could be argued into "Needs" until my parents began to differ on the necessity of certain conveniences in the new house. For instance, bathrooms in those days were new enough to be called a "Want." There were only two in the whole town, and with seven hundred people in the community still unacquainted with plumbing of any kind, how could a bathroom be expected to qualify as a "Need?"

For once Papa's judgment prevailed. He was quite convincing in his arguments that the house would be more salable if it contained a bathroom. (One was considered ample for a five bedroom house.) But Mama was not enthusiastic about this so-called modern convenience. Her reluctance stemmed, I am sure, from pride in her well equipped bedrooms whose marble-topped commodes were graced by flowered china bowls and pitchers.

"Why people should want such a room in the *house,*" she said, "is more than I can understand." And then with spirit, she added, "Certainly, we'll not waste a window on it." And they didn't. The bathroom was placed in the very center of the upstairs. A small vent into the attic and a high window that opened transom-like into my parents' room were all the light and ventilation this step-child of a room received.

Another controversy arose over front and back stairs. Mama had her heart set on an open stairway of polished golden oak ascending from the entrance hall, and Papa acquiesced to that with fairly good grace, but he maintained that the back stairs were not a "Need." Mama argued that they were important in a large house and would save so many steps.

"Besides," she insisted, "it would be such a convenience when callers arrived unexpectedly. I could slip up the back stairs and make myself presentable while Ada admitted the guests. Then I could come serenely down the front stairs to receive them."

Whether due to the feminine logic or to the vision of how pretty Mama would look coming "serenely down the front stairs" Papa's resistance promptly melted and the back stairs were pencilled into the plans.

At the turn of the century it was fashionable for women who aspired to the town's social register to have their day "at home" engraved on their calling cards, an especially welcome custom for Mama after she began to spend so much time helping Papa at the studio. Her day "at home" was the last Thursday in each month but Mama knew that when the move to the new house was made her friends were not going to wait for a special day to make their calls.

Mama won out on the sewing room too. She had a beautiful cabinet sewing machine that was quite the latest thing in equipment. When the top was dropped down and the doors closed, the foot treadle did't show and it looked very much like a small desk. Such a piece of furniture deserved a room of its own, Mama felt, but the argument that won Papa's approval was pure inspiration on her part. She said that such a room would keep all the clutter of sewing in one place.

During my childhood, spring and fall sewing was an established custom in every household. Ready-to-wear clothes were unheard of. Soft, beautiful materials and fine workmanship were far more prized than style by the majority of women. Miss Sophia, our sewing woman, came twice a year — a two weeks' stay each time — and materials were purchased and pattern books studied weeks in advance of her arrival. Papa and I looked upon the advent of Miss Sophia as a mixed blessing. While she was with us there were "Company Meals" and of course we welcomed them, but "Company Manners" were something else. A two-week stretch of being on guard as to what we said or did was a bit trying, to say the least. Mama would warn us again and again to be careful that there might be no occasion for tale-bearing to the next house that Miss Sophia visited. The thought of relegating her and her rituals of cutting, fitting and sewing to one isloated room, leaving the rest of the house free for normal living was too pleasant a prospect for Papa to pass up!

When a room for me came up for consideration in the

house plans, I listened with tense interest. A room of my very own had been the desire of my heart ever since the "Watch Party" at the Steeles that New Year's Eve when the 1800's turned to 1900 and I had been put to bed in Norma's pretty bedroom. Would this "Want" of mine be catalogued as a "Need"? At first the possibility of economizing presented itself — of later turning Ada's room into a room for me. My parents knew that they must arrange for a comfortable room for this faithful helper. She was the daughter of a well-to-do farmer and was always treated as a member of the family. While she worked for the magnificent salary of two dollars a week (and considered herself well paid) yet she ate her meals with us and was always welcome in the sitting room with us in the evening.

The discussion did not last long. There was no way of telling how long help would be needed in the home and now seemed to be the logical time to arrange for a room for me, especially since Mama wanted folding doors between my room and theirs, a requirement that I found rather comforting to contemplate.

Finally the planning was over and the building began. All Strawberry Point watched the progress of this Twentieth Century house as its timbers rose against the Iowa sky and its many comforts and conveniences made their appearance.

The new furnace rated as both a comfort and convenience. There would be no more stoves to put up every fall and take down in the spring, and this huge octopus, with tentacle-like pipes stretching to the basement ceiling in every direction would keep the new house warm and comfortable during the most rigid Iowa winter.

141

Another modern wonder and the cause of raised eyebrows, was the hot and cold running water in not only the kitchen but downstairs lavatory and upstairs bathroom. The lavatory was not too complete because even farsighted Papa could see little need for a toilet downstairs when accommodations were adequate at the end of the arbor-covered walk in the back yard.

Many a housewife sighed over the hardwood floors when they made their appearance. Vacuum Cleaners were decades away and the rag carpets of the "nineties" were a task to keep clean.

The lighting in the new house was another innovation, and quite the envy of the whole town. Downstairs there were chandeliers in every room and the light from them was dazzling — far brighter than either electricity or gas, which we knew nothing about. These Acetylene lights, as they were called, would splutter and emit a not too pleasant odor before they suddenly flaired up into a brilliance that was overpowering. The upstairs was lit by the softer, more familiar glow of kerosene lamps, a highly satisfactory arrangement, we thought.

March merged into April, April into May, and May into June before the new house was finally finished. It was not the finest perhaps, architecturally speaking, but one that surely reflected in many ways the changes that the new century would soon be bringing to everyone. When we moved down maple-lined Main Street the summer of 1903 we left the Victorian Era (and much of its charm) behind us. But the New House stood sturdy, forthright and loved — a miracle of comfort and convenience.

17

THE CHRISTENING

THE FIRST week in the new house was a time of bustling activity. Mama and Ada worked from early morning until late in the evening, hanging curtains and pictures, placing and replacing furniture and getting the household into running order.

All our best furniture — the dignified secretary, the golden oak center table and newest chairs — as well as the crisp new lace curtains and prettiest rug went into the "front room," as our parlor was now called. This room was to be the one reserved for callers and for special occasions. The older, more comfortable furniture plus the piano, the music cabinet, Papa's guitar and Mama's mandolin settled down in the adjacent sitting room where family activities would now center. An outside entrance to a side porch promised to route family traffic through this room, thus saving wear and tear on the front room and entrance hall.

I was assigned the task of settling my own room and was delighted to have the opportunity to arrange my treasures to my own satisfaction. I decorated the lace curtains with prized Sunday School cards and perfect spelling papers. My paper dolls I housed in two strawberry crates upended in a corner of the room. The bookshelf for my meager but well worn library of favorites — "The Five Little Peppers," "The Gypsy Breynton Books" and a few others — I placed by my white iron bed. A bedside table, a curtained dry-goods box that served as a dresser and a small rocker, completed my room furnishings.

Because of the wide double doorway into my parents' room I had very little privacy but when night time came this open doorway was quite a solace to a little girl who had slept in a trundle bed at their feet for so many years. And was I grateful for the feeling of "nearness" the night of the burglar alarm!

As soon as we were settled, Ada went home for a short visit and well-earned rest. The first night after she left, Papa and I had gone to bed when Mama returned to the kitchen on some long since forgotten errand. I was almost asleep when I heard her scurrying up the front stairs and heard her hoarse whisper:

"George, George, there's a burglar in the kitchen!"

By the amused and lazy tone of Papa's voice when he answered her, I knew he was not much concerned.

"What," he said, "a burglar in Strawberry Point?"

146

But when he turned and saw Mama's face, he was out of bed with one bound. Rescuing the lamp from her trembling hand, he set it carefully on the dresser, and taking both her hands in his, he propelled her gently to a chair.

"Now sit down," he said in a quiet, matter-of-fact voice, "and tell us exactly what happened."

Striving hard for self-control, Mama answered in a stage whisper, "I was hurrying across the kitchen, when I saw the cellar-way door move. Someone must have stepped behind it just as I came in!" Her eyes were big with terror at the very thought.

Without another word, Papa picked up the handlamp and started for the stairs.

Mama's voice was no longer a whisper when she realized his purpose.

"George, what are you thinking of to go down those stairs unarmed! Don't go. I beg of you, don't go!"

Mama could be melodramatic on occasion.

"If I don't go and settle this thing," he said, "you won't sleep a wink all night."

A statement we recognized as the truth.

Mama was afraid to go down again, but more afraid to remain upstairs without Papa. So the procession formed. Papa led, holding the handlamp aloft, his generous two hundred pounds scantily clad in his abbreviated nightshirt; his unruly red hair standing on end. Mama came next, still pale and with eyes that were black pools of fear. I brought up the rear, clutching Mama's calico wrapper and not at all sure that the rear with its shadowy darkness was the safest place to be.

Slowly we descended the stairs, stopping every few steps

147

while Papa lifted the lamp higher to peer into the shadow ahead of us. Silently we continued across the downstairs hall and through the dining room. At the kitchen door, Papa paused deliberately and fastened back the newfangled swinging door on the dining room side. Then we continued, single file, straight across the kitchen to the cellar-way. Papa pushed back the door with force and it yielded readily to his touch. Nothing there. To my horror, he went on down the stairs into the dark abyss of the cellar. The dim lamplight, as Papa swung the lamp about, showed the cellar windows tightly locked and everything shipshape.

On the return trip to the kitchen I didn't wait to be last. I was sure there was more safety in the familiar kitchen than in the eerie shadows of the cellar. As we stood in the center of the kitchen floor, Papa's face wore a puzzled frown. Nothing had been disturbed — that was evident. But Mama was looking apprehensively at the door to the back stairs. A reasonable explanation must be found to satisfy her. Suddenly his face cleared. Setting the lamp on the kitchen table, he stepped to the door that led into the dining room. Releasing the lever that held the door back to the wall, he gave the swinging door a sudden violent push — and in the tightly closed kitchen we watched fascinated as the cellar door began to move as though swung by an invisible hand.

As the full impact of what had happened dawned upon us, the new kitchen fairly rang with relieved laughter. At that very moment the new house suddenly became a home. The sound of laughter seemed a fitting way to christen it for we knew instinctively that this home was going to be a very happy one.

THE kitchen in the new house was a miracle of convenience. Ada, our hired girl, was very proud of the white
porcelain sink with its long drainboard and she kept it shiny
clean. Too, she liked the hot and cold running water and the
pump that brought up the soft water from the reservoir in the
basement, and she would point out with pride the new kitchen
cabinet with its built-in flour and sugar bins. With so much
equipment, there was no room for Mama's old rocking chair —
but no one cared. The kitchen was no longer a family gathering
place but a bustling workshop where almost anything was liable
to be created.

151

One afternoon I came home from school to find Mama and her friend, Bertha Harrington, manufacturing Cold Cream! Cosmetics had not yet appeared in the stores when Mama and Bertha concocted that first successful batch of facial cream. They had found the recipe in a newspaper. Just how it was made I do not now remember, but from the bottles of rose water and the box of almond meal on the kitchen table and the array of kitchen pans on the sink drainboard, I am sure it must have been a complicated process.

It was about this same time that Mama (and Bertha, too) began, surreptitiously, to use face powder. I was not supposed to know it. Mama kept the box well hidden in the back of her top dresser drawer. Such a vanity was still frowned upon by many good people and Mama herself was not entirely convinced that "nice" women should use such a prop to their beauty. "Handsome is as handsome does" was the popular adage of that day Anyway, Mama was never guilty of allowing a single trace of powder to show and carefully dusted her face just enough to remove the shine.

Our buxom, country-bred hired girl had a complexion that was the envy of Mama and all her friends. It was supposed that Ada's rosy cheeks were the result of her wholesome, country upbringing, and perhaps they were at one time. But one day I came upon her unexpectedly as she stood before the kitchen mirror industriously applying color to her cheeks with a moistened bit of rose colored netting that she had salvaged from the top of a peach basket! (In those days fruits were sold in baskets that were covered with a coarse, colored netting to protect and also enhance the color of the fruit.) In front of

Ada on the kitchen table lay a whole pile of these colored nets — and the secret of her fresh beauty was in my hands. Of course I was sworn to secrecy then and there, but I'm afraid that from that day on, I was guilty of blackmail. Many a delicacy from the kitchen came my way that I never would have received had I not at opportune moments referred to Ada's beautiful complexion.

I think it was about the time that Mama and Bertha began to try out fancy salad and dessert recipes in our kitchen that gelatin in its refined form made its debut — or at least came into common use. In my grandmother's time the jellied recipies were made with calf's feet jelly and isinglass. The wording of one such recipe taken from her old cook book is quaint:—

FRUIT IN JELLY

Put into a basin half a pint of clear calf's feet jelly, and when it is set and stiff, lay in three fine peaches and a bunch of grapes with the stalk upwards. Put over them a few vine leaves, and then fill up your bowl with jelly. Let it stand till the next day and then set your basin to the brim in hot water. When you percieve it gives way from the basin, lay your dish over it, turn your jelly carefully out, and serve to table."

Queer ingredients were used to color jellies in those remote days. In Grandma's recipe for Orange Jelly, she suggests that after the isinglass, water, sugar and fruit juice are boiled together it is well to add, "any dried crocus flowers to give it a fine yellow tinge." A recipe for "Blanc Mange" calls for the juice of spinach to make it green! And in making jelly, "you must color red with cochineal and blue with syrup of violets."

Some of my most prized recipes are the ones Bertha Harrington gave to Mama in the early 1900's. She was a marvelous cook and loved to try out new ideas, and very often they

(Bertha and Mama) would experiment in our convenient kitchen. On one recipe is inscribed this nostalgic message:—

> "Ruby, I wonder if you will remember the day I helped you make this Grape Sherbet when you were entertaining "Thimbles" at your new home. Those were the 'good old days' — the happiest ever.

Bertha and Mama often entertained together, not only at "Thimble Club" but at evening dinner parties as well. These rather formal dinners did not meet with Papa's approval. He was a plain man who liked plain, well-cooked meals. He disliked anything that, as he said, smacked of "putting on airs." And he was known to remark plaintively that he did like something more substantial to eat than "humming-birds' wings."

On one of these occasions, when an unusually large number of guests had been invited, Mama and Bertha decided to seat them at small, candle-lit tables for four. When the place cards were put out in the afternoon, Mama was careful to see that Papa was placed with three of his best friends. That night when he was dressing for dinner, Mama was able to side track his usual complaints by assuring him that he would be in congenial company. He went down to dinner somewhat mollified and in much better humor than usual.

All went well while the first course was being served. Papa, in an expansive mood, was already deep in conversation when the beef consommé was placed before him. It was something entirely new — this clear, thin broth served in dainty cups, but Papa gave it scant attention. Thinking the "girls" had decided to serve the tea for a first course, he resigned himself to this new "notion" and sprinkled his consommé liberally with sugar!

When he tasted his "tea" things began to happen. He choked. He spluttered. And all of his pent-up exasperation at his wife and her innovative ideas was in his voice when he called across the room:

"Ruby, what in thunder is the matter with the tea?"

For one awful moment Mama sat speechless and petrified — her beautiful party, as she thought, in ruins. Why, oh why, hadn't she remembered to warn him about the consommé! But when the startled guests realized what had happened and saw the wry face and outraged look of this usually patient man, they burst into gales of laughter.

When order was restored, Mama found to her surprise and great relief that all formality had completely evaporated. Everyone was relaxed and gay, and the party was well on its way to success.

The new kitchen was a beehive of activity for many a party during the years we lived in the new house. Even though I was never sure whether I would find cold cream or consommé being manufactured there, yet I always knew that this "heart of the home" would be pulsing with action and that something exciting would be going on there.

19

THE WHEELS OF PROGRESS
ROLL IN STRAWBERRY POINT

THE CHRISTMAS of 1903 Papa surprised us with a Graphophone. As the little black cylinders revolved and the music came forth from the morning-glory horn, we sat entranced. Never had we heard anything like this.

Strawberry Point could boast of a "dance band," occasionally road shows brought with them a musician or two, and once the "Cherry Sisters" regaled us with "Ta-ra-ra-ra Boom-de-ay." But mostly we fed our hunger for music by providing it ourselves on the piano in the parlor. Now with the advent of this wonderfully magic "music box," we heard really good music. How thrilled we were and how our feet tapped to the inspiring strains of Sousa's marches played by his famous band!

than risk an encounter which might very well end in a runaway.

There were no side doors on the touring cars in those days. The center back seat lifted up, and when the door at the rear of the car was opened, a step dropped down. After the back-seat occupants had filed in, the center seat was let down again. The car had a right-hand drive, and the crank (no starter, of course) was on the driver's side. There were wicker baskets along the sides of the car to carry the luggage and wraps. The top, a canopy affair, was never raised except when a rainstorm threatened. When it was up, it interferred with the speed of the car — and we did so enjoy skimming along the country roads at the thrilling speed of twenty miles an hour!

The summer of 1903, Uncle Charlie invited our family to accompany him and his family on a trip to western Iowa. That was real pioneering. There was no place to buy gasoline except at hardware stores, and not a repair man to be found in all the two hundred miles we traveled. The tires were poor, so loose they slipped, often pulling off the valve stems. We soon resigned ourselves to at least a half-dozen punctures a day.

Another daily problem on the trip was that of runaways. Never a day that I did not hide my head in Mama's lap while some beautiful horse reared, balked, or ran for his life. Uncle was very quick to stop the car and give a helping hand. One time this almost proved disastrous for us. The frightened horse became so confused that he headed for the car instead of away from it, and we all sat petrified while he endeavored to join us in the back seat!

Cars were a real curiosity that summer of 1903. When we arrived in a town, a crowd would gather almost before we stopped, asking all kinds of questions. Farmers would telephone ahead to their neighbors that an automobile was coming, and often whole families lined up at the fence to watch us go by.

Our destination was Marcus, Iowa, where Grandfather Roe's brother lived. Except for the two days we were there, we spent the full two weeks we had planned to be away just traveling or attempting to travel the two hundred miles.

The inner workings of this huge machine were undependable too, and neither Uncle nor Papa was mechanically inclined. At the little town of Newell, on the return trip, the car rebelled completely and we were stranded there until repairs arrived from the factory.

In spite of the difficulties we experienced on the trip, however, Papa was still very enthusiastic about this new invention. With spirits undampened by Uncle Charlie's troubles, Papa began to talk about the *need* of a car to drive to his branch galleries, so Mama and I were not at all surprised when one day he returned from Cedar Rapids driving an Oldsmobile roadster. It looked very much like our old buggy, execpt that it was steered by a long lever.

Papa was accompanied home by a young mechanic who departed by train the following day. We watched him leave with many misgivings, and our fears were well grounded. The car proved every bit as temperamental as Uncle Charlie's model. However, when it was on good behavior, the car sped along so smoothly and swiftly (to us who were accustomed to the leisurely pace of Black Bess) that all the trouble it caused us was quickly forgotten.

The dirt roads were definitely a drawback to pleasant driving.

At that time there wasn't a paved road in all Iowa, nor a paved street in Strawberry Point. Usually we came in from a drive completely covered with fine white dust. Mama and I always wore thin coats (dusters they were aptly called) to protect our dresses, and our hats were securely anchored to our heads with flowing veils.

Probably the worst experience of all was to be caught out in a rain that turned the roads into rivers. If we were unfortunate enough to be on a clay hill, then the wheels began to spin and we knew we must throw ourselves on the mercy of a nearby farmer. He came with his team, hauled us into his yard, and usually offered us the hospitality of his home for the night.

Papa's sisters were not too eager to ride with either of their brothers. But one day, when Aunt Eleanor was visiting us, Papa talked her into going for a "little spin." All went well at first, but it was not long before we heard the ominous skip - skip - skip - which prophesied trouble. From the expression on Papa's face and his listening attitude, Aunt knew he was concerned about something.

"What's bothering you, George?" she shouted. (One had to shout to be heard above the roar of those ancient automobiles. They sounded like threshing-machines.)

"One of the cylinders is missing," Papa shouted in reply.

"Oh, that's too bad," she sympathized. "Do you suppose you might have left it in the gar'ij?"

Aunt Eleanor never quite lived down that remark. But at least she had remembered to call the barn a garage — an achievement the rest of us did not accomplish for some time.

20

WHEN PAPA RAN THE PICTURE SHOW

SOMETIMES I cannot help but wonder what Father, rugged individualist that he was, would think of the world we now live in — with its Social Security, its multitude of taxes and its paternal government. Papa, who could never understand how, as he said, a man could sell himself into the slavery of a salaried job; Papa, who did not even believe in life insurance!

"Why should I let another man save my money for me?" he would say. "If a Company is willing to gamble that I'll live to a ripe old age, I'll gamble that way, too, and handle the money for my own funeral expenses."

The Roe Photograph Studio, from the time I was born until

I graduated from college, was our bread and butter, but not the cake or the frosting on it. That came from Papa's "Deals." When he came home with a special glint in his eye and seemed in unusually good spirits we knew a deal was in the making. He loved to buy, sell, or trade anything and everything that came his way. Mama and I, he was fond of saying, were all that he had that did not have prices attached. Houses, farms, bankrupt stocks of goods, rooming houses, hotels — all came and went — always at a substantial profit for Papa. And once he even bought a motion-picture theater.

I was a girl in high school when the cinema arrived in our town. Dreamland was a small theater but it was highly successful until a competitor moved in just a block away. The Orpheum, as the new movie house was called, was twice as large as Dreamland and far more beautiful with its comfortable loge seats and large foyer, but Papa shook his head.

"It won't last a year," he predicted.

When Mama questioned him as to why he was so sure, he replied, "The price of admission. Imagine charging *ten cents* for a moving-picture show!"

Dreamland charged only five cents, and since the shows were about the same in character it was not long before Papa's prophecy came true. When the newness wore off, people flocked back to the cheaper cinema.

I don't remember just how long the new theater held out, but I do remember well the night Papa came home with the special "gleam" in his eye and announced that he had bought the Orpheum.

Mama was far from pleased. "What on earth," she said,

"are you going to do with a bankrupt moving-picture theater?"

"Run it," he said laconically.

And run it he did, for three long months. When the theater was restored to its former, garish beauty, Papa opened with quite a fanfare for those days. He hired a young woman as pianist who could really "play the pictures." The piano under her expert fingers thundered with the storm, sobbed with the deserted heroine, and marched to victory with the uniformed hero. Papa hired another town girl with a pleasing voice to sing a popular song under a spotlight as a prologue to the film. The words of the song were thrown on the screen and the audience was invited to join in on the chorus.

But what really put the theater back into the good graces of the townspeople was the price of admission. It had been lowered to five cents.

Mama was concerned about that. Summer had arrived and in Iowa the summer nights are often hotter than the days. Air-conditioning was unheard of, and to gamble with the weather, Mama thought, was reckless to say the least. But all summer long the crowds continued. People came with their palm-leaf fans, but they came.

By midsummer, Mama was willing to admit that Papa's judgment had been vindicated, but it was several more weeks before she recognized in the theater an excellent opportunity to improve her social status in the community.

That summer there had been a perfect whirl of garden parties, and Mama had become indebted (as she said) to practically everyone in town. It finally occurred to her that she had better pay off her social obligations while the weather was still warm enough so that she too could entertain outdoors on the lawn.

One evening she sat soberly chewing her pencil as she worked on her guest list. "If it weren't for the size of this party I'd have it in the house even if the weather is hot — just to be different," she remarked with a sigh. "I do wish I could think of something, at least in the way of entertainment, that would be out of the ordinary."

Papa looked up from his paper with a twinkle in his eye. "Why not have a theater party?" he said, not expecting to be taken seriously.

"What a perfectly marvelous idea!" Mama cried, her eyes shining with excitement. "If I can only get Lil Kuney to go in with me!" and she jumped from her chair and ran to the telephone.

Kuney's Imperial Concert Orchestra was well known in Iowa and that summer was playing on a Chautauqua circuit. Will Kuney, the popular Conductor, and his wife Lillian were childhood friends of my parents. It was not hard to guess what Mama had in mind when she made her telephone call.

"If we should choose a date for our party when the orchestra is playing in the neighborhood," she said (thinking aloud as she talked on the phone), "perhaps Will could persuade the men to furnish the music." Warming to the idea the longer they talked, Mama continued, "We can have a morning musicale. A sort of breakfast — early enough so we can use the Orpheum and before the heat of the day."

Here Papa interrupted to say that positively they would have to be out of the theater by noon. But such details Mama brushed aside. She could handle them, she knew. She loved to organize affairs of any kind and this novel idea was going to give her talent plenty of scope.

The orchestra cooperated beautifully, and the program grew of its own momentum. It was a simple matter to draft talented friends for the occasion — young women who were delighted to have the opportunity to sing with a "name" band.

The stage was decorated with ferns and garden flowers and, as our town newspaper faithfully reported, was a "bower of beauty." The auditorium, too, wore a really festive air with lighted Japanese lanterns suspended from the ceiling.

The four hundred guests were invited for nine o'clock in the morning — an unheard-of hour for a party in our small town, but there wasn't a single regret. No one was going to miss an affair that was such an innovation as this one promised to be.

The food was the big problem — how to serve it, and keep the hot things hot and the cold things cold. This was Mama's responsibility and she managed by persuading active, nimble-footed high school friends of mine (dressed as usherettes) to act as waitresses. After the program was over, they promptly took up their appointed stations and deftly passed out the delicious "brunch." It had been prepared by the hostesses and transported to the theater well packed in ice. The drink arrived piping hot from the restaurant next door.

Cinderella-like, the theater returned to its prosaic everyday appearance on the stroke of twelve. Papa, good-naturedly, had a cleanup crew ready to take over promptly after the departure of the last guest. The whole morning had gone like clockwork and the hostesses were all aglow with satisfaction. They had given "one of the most pleasant and original social functions of the season."

My own prestige, too, reached a new high that summer, for I issued complimentary tickets for matinees with a lavish hand. All in all, we considered the theater one of Papa's most satisfactory ventures. In the fall he sold this new plaything and made a thousand dollars on the sale.

21

THE WIDENING HORIZON
WE SAY GOODBYE TO STRAWBERRY POINT

WHEN Uncle Charles, Aunt Belle and my older cousin, Floyd, left Arlington to make a home in Iowa's capitol city, Des Moines, they had my deepest sympathy. I thought Strawberry Point with its tree-lined streets a far prettier place to live than Arlington, but life in any little town, to my way of thinking, was far superior to life in a large, crowded metropolis.

In our small town of Strawberry Point, life flowed along easily. Everyone knew everyone else as generation followed generation. Girls like my mother, who were born on Main Street and grew up there, were satisfied and content to marry and establish their own homes on this same maple-canopied street.

These old trees must have been planted by the men who founded the little town almost fifty years before the turn of the century, for in my childhood — the first decade of the 1900's — these tall sentinels were already reaching for the sky. In the spring, decked in their fresh green leaves, they were a vision of lacy loveliness; in the summer their arched branches created cool canyons to sauter through; in the fall, the leaves, vividly colored by Jack Frost, were breath-taking in their splendor; and, when the trees wore their winter garments of ice and snow, they were a fairyland of shining beauty. How could anyone ask for a prettier place to live, I often wondered. Probably I was made more keenly appreciative of the advantages of small-town living because of my two excursions into the world of city streets, both unhappy experiences.

When I was a very little girl, probably not over eight years of age, my parents and I visited Cousin Edie, Aunt Alma's daughter, who had married and moved to Dubuque, a thriving city on the Mississippi River. That was my first acquaintance with city pavements, tall buildings, crowded streets and the general confusion and accelerated pace of city living. The impression I gained was not a pleasant one. I remember being hurried along the busy streets, past people with unfriendly faces, and of feeling overwhelmed by a great sense of loneliness and by a nameless fear of the whole, sorry picture. On the street where Edie lived there was not a tree or a a spear of grass. So *this,* I thought, is city-living. How I pitied my poor, grown-up cousin who was forced by circumstances to live in such a dreadful place!

Again, when I was eleven, Uncle Charlie took me with him to Cedar Rapids. The train ride — the longest I had ever taken — was exciting and fun. But when we arrived in the city I was assailed by the same frightening sense that I had felt on the memorable trip to Dubuque — a conviction that I was in an unfriendly world. I can still remember how I clung to Uncle's hand as we waited for a cab. What if I should become separated from him and find myself alone in this big, strange place. The very thought struck terror to my inmost being. Then and there I determined that if I ever arrived home safely I would never, never again leave beautiful, secure, friendly Strawberry Point.

But the spring of my first year in High School, my horizon suddenly widened. There came an invitation from our relatives in Des Moines for us to visit them in their new home and enjoy the graduation festivities on the campus at Drake University.

With the background of my two previous adventures, it is not surprising that the trip to Des Moines was undertaken without much enthusiasm on my part. In fact, I was totally unprepared for the delights in store for us.

Perhaps my added years made me more appreciative of and interested in the crowded days of sight-seeing. The city streets no longer depressed or intimidated me as we viewed them from the safety of Uncle Charles' luxurious automobile.

The highlight of the trip, the one that has stayed with me down the years, was the graduation exercises on the beautiful campus of the University. In that hour was born the desire to some day march that same path in a cap and gown. The music department even then was outstanding and we heard a Song Recital that stirred within me ambitions never before awakened. One young woman sang so beautifully, so simply, that my throat ached from holding back the tears. Oh, to be able to sing like that!

The day after the recital we returned home, but something had changed — something within me. Never again was I quite content to drift with the pleasant current of small-town life. My parents, too, shared my awakening for it was less than a year later that they began to consider plans that changed all our lives.

An opportunity presented itself for Papa to buy a photograph studio in a flourishing Iowa town several times larger than Strawberry Point. This change of residence would mean that Papa could give up his branch galleries and devote all his time to the one studio. It would mean for me better advantages in music and school. But it also meant tearing up the very roots of our pleasant life in Strawberry Point — giving up the long-time friends and the new home. For Mama, this change would mean leaving the street where she was born and where she had lived all her thirty-five years — the giving up of the only way of life that she had ever known.

Strangely enough, it was Papa and I, not Mama, who hesitated at the thought of leaving the familiar landmarks and good friends. It was Mama who comforted and encouraged us.

"There is another home waiting for us," she said, "and soon

there will be new friends. Let's go forward, and not hang onto the past."

Mama lived by copybook maxims and always had a wise one to bolster herself up in every family crisis. This time she quoted Emerson: "Hitch your wagon to a star. A star," she reminded us, "is not a mere celestial body, but a spirited race horse."

"Maybe we're ready for a faster pace now — for a quickening stream of life. Let's reach out for the world. Let's widen our horizons. We'll still have Strawberry Point. We'll keep it safely in our hearts!"

Papa nodded thoughtfully in agreement. I looked out wistfully at the maples lining Main Street. Like the roots of those huge trees, my small-town memories and loyalties ran deep and wide. Come what may, part of me, I knew, would never, ever leave Strawberry Point!

22

ENVOY

YOUTH'S earnest questions, cited in the Foreword, have been answered in the important values underlying the stories, not in the simple events recorded. Many of the foes lurking in ambush today were unknown to our forefathers, but the same qualities of thought that defeated the enemy of yesterday are equal to the emergencies of today.

As we treasure these values they will become visible in our every-day life. And how we need their steadying influence! Materiality with its tempting promises besieges us on every side and material success stands elusively at the end of a retreating rainbow.

Perhaps the most difficult adjustment to the life of the modern world has fallen on the man who loves to farm — who carries the blood of pioneers in his veins. Those who would wrest a living from the land must do so amidst a forest of subdivision signs or under the black clouds of Big Business' frowning disapproval.

Not long ago I walked down a country lane and across well-kept Iowa fields that once had belonged to my pioneering grandfather. I was following my husband and our host (my cousin) as they started on an inspection tour of the cornfields.

As I loitered to pick the wild roses growing along the fences, to whistle to a bobwhite and to search the berry bushes that grew wild along the sides of the lane, I found myself lagging farther and farther behind the men. Their voices grew fainter as the distance between us widened, and suddenly I was alone in all that beautiful stillness that is the country.

Quietly I stood there, drinking in the fragrance of the clover-scented air and listening to the small sounds that seemed to accent the cathedral-like peace of the countryside: the tinkle of a cowbell on the still air, the hum of the bees as they worked in the clover, the song of my bird friends in the hedges. Oh, it was a prime day, unmarred by a single dissonance.

On a little knoll above the meadow, I glimpsed the white farmhouse that Grandfather built in 1857, as it nestled in the dooryard maples. I remembered the story of its building and how Grandfather hauled the lumber from Dubuque — a city fifty miles away — to build this house that was still sheltering his family four generations later.

Such a home expresses a permanence that is fast disappearing

184

today. Of course, the small, family size farm is not Utopia but it has been for three hundred years the back-bone of the nation. It would be well to weigh values before country living is exchanged completely for city streets. The city worships at the shrine of standardization while the country fosters the individual. Many of our greatest men lived their childhood on the land.

And small towns, too, have had to adjust to change. The Strawberry Point of 1900 has completely disappeared. Not but what a good Iowa road map could quickly direct us to this still beautiful little town, but Hollywood, television, airplanes and automobiles have transformed it as they have every town and city in the nation. Peck's Harness Shop, along with Black Bess, has vanished. A gasoline station now graces (?) the Stearns Place and its popular side yard at the corner of Main Street and Maxim's Lane. The proud Franklin Hotel, that opened its doors to the lilting strains of "A Bicycle Built For Two" (played by Cousin Harry's popular Mandolin Club) has now given way to convenient motels and the faster pace set by the salesmen who now travel by plane and car. All of this we must accept in a changing world. But, happily, we have kept the Strawberry Point we knew where all that was good and right and beautiful in the life of Yesterday must be kept — "safely in our hearts."